Lecture Notes in Computer Science 13755

More information about this series at https://link.springer.com/bookseries/558

John S. H. Baxter · Islem Rekik · Roy Eagleson ·
Luping Zhou · Tanveer Syeda-Mahmood ·
Hongzhi Wang · Mustafa Hajij (Eds.)

Ethical and Philosophical Issues in Medical Imaging, Multimodal Learning and Fusion Across Scales for Clinical Decision Support, and Topological Data Analysis for Biomedical Imaging

1st International Workshop, EPIMI 2022
12th International Workshop, ML-CDS 2022
2nd International Workshop, TDA4BiomedicalImaging
Held in Conjunction with MICCAI 2022
Singapore, September 18–22, 2022
Proceedings

Springer

Editors
John S. H. Baxter (iD)
Université de Rennes 1
Rennes, France

Roy Eagleson (iD)
Western University
London, ON, Canada

Tanveer Syeda-Mahmood (iD)
IBM Almaden Research Center
San Jose, CA, USA

Mustafa Hajij
University of San Francisco
San Francisco, CA, USA

Islem Rekik (iD)
Imperial College London
London, UK

Luping Zhou (iD)
University of Sydney
Sydney, NSW, Australia

Hongzhi Wang
IBM Almaden Research Center
San Jose, CA, USA

ISSN 0302-9743   ISSN 1611-3349 (electronic)
Lecture Notes in Computer Science
ISBN 978-3-031-23222-0   ISBN 978-3-031-23223-7 (eBook)
https://doi.org/10.1007/978-3-031-23223-7

This Springer imprint is published by the registered company Springer Nature Switzerland AG
The registered company address is: Gewerbestrasse 11, 6330 Cham, Switzerland

EPIMI Preface

The human body lies at the intersection of both scientific complexity and humanistic interest, leading to the unique position of medicine in the sciences and thus the philosophy of medicine in the wider philosophical tradition. Medical imaging in particular, as the beneficiary of numerous advances in fields ranging from quantum physics to computer science, has advanced well ahead of its philosophical and bioethical underpinnings. Although it is not uncommon for scientific disciplines to do so in general (e.g. quantum physics had developed for decades in the late 1800s and early 1900s before questions of its interpretation were first published in 1926) medical imaging's association with the human body gives it an additional humanistic dimension and its growing use in medicine as a whole makes the investigation of this dimension more pressing. In addition, many tools and concepts have evolved to assist medical imaging, notably through image computing and computer-assisted interventions, which come with their own philosophical and ethical implications regarding the fair allocation of resources and equitable definitions of accuracy, but also regarding more abstract questions in epistemology, semiotics, and ownership. To draw an analogy, a distinct philosophy of medical imaging is to the philosophy of medicine as medical imaging itself is to medicine: it shares the same end but uses a distinctly different plethora of means; it exists as both a sub-discipline and a separate one.

The first workshop on Ethical and Philosophical Issues in Medical Imaging (EPIMI 2022) was a foray into this discipline and began to fill what we see as a gap in the connection between the MICCAI community and the philosophy of medicine community. EPIMI 2022 included five short papers about various humanistic aspects of medical image computing and computer-assisted interventions. These papers were selected from seven submissions after double-blind review by at least three independent reviewers, followed by an additional author rebuttal. The first two accepted papers investigate bioethical questions concerning the use of machine learning, specifically system security and racial fairness, through a mixed theoretical/empirical approach. The third is a philosophical examination of the values underlying machine learning research. The final two papers address public perception of digital health technologies in an under-represented population as well as how to involve clinicians in developing these technologies. Overall, they represent some of the foremost humanistic concerns and philosophical preoccupations of those working in the field.

Lastly, we would like to thank the authors and reviewers, as well as all those who attended EPIMI 2022 and contributed to the fruitful and critical discussions there. You have all been a part in advancing philosophical inquiry into medical image computing and computer-assisted interventions.

September 2022

John S. H. Baxter
Islem Rekik
Roy Eagleson
Luping Zhou

EPIMI Organization

Program and Organizing Committee

John S. H. Baxter   University of Rennes, France
Islem Rekik   Imperial College London, UK
Roy Eagleson   Western University, Canada
Luping Zhou   University of Sydney, Australia

Steering Committee

Elisabetta Lalumera   University of Bologna, Italy
Pierre Jannin   University of Rennes, France
Terry M. Peters   Western University, Canada
Dinggang Shen   Shanghai Technical University, China

ML-CDS Preface

On behalf of the organizing committee, we welcome you to the proceedings of the Workshop on Multimodal Learning and Fusion Across Scales for Clinical Decision Support (ML-CDS) held in person at MICCAI 2022 in Singapore. This is the 12th edition of our workshop, which has been held annually at MICCAI since 2009. Overall, the goal of this series of workshops has been to bring together medical image analysis and machine learning researchers with clinicians to tackle the important challenges of acquiring and interpreting multimodality medical data at multiple scales for clinical decision support and treatment planning, and to present and discuss latest developments in the field.

The previous workshops on this topic have been well-received at MICCAI, specifically in Strasbourg (2021), Lima (2020), Shenzen (2019), Granada (2018), Quebec City (2017), Athens (2016), Munich (2015), Nagoya (2013), Nice (2012), Toronto (2011), and London (2009). Continuing on the momentum built by these workshops, this year's edition focused on integrating diagnostic imaging, pathology imaging, and genomic datasets for diagnosis and treatment planning treating clinical decision support on a holistic basis.

We received three submissions which all underwent a double-blind peer-review process, with each submission reviewed by at least two independent reviewers. Based on the review scores and comments, all three papers were accepted for presentation at the workshop and inclusion in this Springer LNCS volume. We would like to thank the authors for their submissions and all the Program Committee members for handling the submissions with professional judgements and constructive comments.

With less than 5% of medical image analysis techniques translating to clinical practice, workshops on this topic have helped raise the awareness of our field to clinical practitioners. The approach taken in the workshop is to scale it to large collections of patient data exposing interesting issues of multimodal learning and its specific use in clinical decision support by practicing physicians. The ultimate impact of these methods can be judged when they begin to affect treatment planning in clinical practice.

With the introduction of a clinical program at MICCAI 2023 as part of the main conference, and the appointment of clinical chairs, the goals of the workshop on spreading the awareness of this topic within the MICCAI community have effectively been reached. We would like to thank MICCAI for supporting the workshop through the years and look forward to another successful edition of the workshop in 2023.

September 2022

Tanveer Syeda-Mahmood
Anant Madabhushi
Hayit Greenspan
Hongzhi Wang

ML-CDS Organization

Program Chairs

Tanveer Syeda-Mahmood   IBM Research - Almaden, USA
Anant Madabhushi   Case Western Reserve University, USA
Hayit Greenspan   Tel-Aviv University, Israel
Hongzhi Wang   IBM Research - Almaden, USA

Program Committee

Amir Amini   University of Louisville, USA
Sameer Antani   National Library of Medicine, USA
Rivka Colen   Andersen Research Center, USA
Niharika D'Souza   IBM Research - Almaden, USA
Keyvan Farahani   National Cancer Institute, USA
Alejandro Frangi   University of Leeds, UK
Guido Gerig   New York University, USA
Andrea Giovannini   IBM Research - Zurich, Switzerland
David Gutman   Emory University, USA
Allan Halpern   Memorial Sloan-Kettering Research Center, USA
Ghassan Hamarneh   Simon Fraser University, Canada
Jayshree Kalpathy-Cramer   Massachusetts General Hospital, USA
Ron Kikinis   Harvard University, USA
Georg Langs   Medical University of Vienna, Austria
B. Manjunath   University of California, Santa Barbara, USA
Dimitris Metaxas   Rutgers University, USA
Nikos Paragios   CentraleSupélec, France
Daniel Racoceanu   Sorbonne University, France
Eduardo Romero   Universidad Nationale Colombia, Colombia
Daniel Rubin   Stanford University, USA
Russ Taylor   Johns Hopkins University, USA
Agma Traina   Sao Paulo University, Brazil
Max Viergewer   Utrecht University, The Netherlands
Chun I Wong   IBM Research - Almaden, USA
Sean Zhou   Shanghai United Imaging Intelligence, USA

TDA Preface

TDA4BiomedicalImaging 2022 was the second International Workshop on Topological Data Analysis for Biomedical Imaging. The TDA4BiomedicalImaging 2022 proceedings contain three high-quality papers which were selected from a group of nine submissions through a rigorous double-blind peer review process with three reviewers per paper.

Recent years have witnessed an increasing interest in the role topology plays in machine learning and data science. Topology offers a collection of techniques and tools that have matured to a field known today as topological data analysis (TDA). TDA provides a general and multi-purpose set of robust tools that have shown excellent performance in several real-world applications. These tools are naturally applicable to numerous types of data including images, point clouds, graphs, meshes, time-varying data, and more. TDA techniques have been increasingly used with other techniques such as deep learning to increase the performance, and generalizability, of a generic learning task. Further, the properties of the topological tools allow the identification of complex relationships and separation of signals that are hidden in the data from noise. Finally, topological methods naturally lend themselves to visualization rendering them useful for tasks that require interpretability and explainability.

All these properties of topological-based methods strongly motivate the adoption of TDA tools in various applications and domains including neuroscience, bioscience, biomedicine, and medical imaging. This workshop focused on using TDA techniques to enhance the performance, generalizability, efficiency, and explainability of the current methods applied to medical data. In particular, the workshop focused on using TDA tools solely or combined with other computational techniques (e.g., feature engineering and deep learning) to analyze medical data including images/videos, sounds, physiological, texts, and sequence data. The combination of TDA and other computational approaches is more effective in summarizing, analyzing, quantifying, and visualizing complex medical data. This workshop brought together mathematicians, biomedical engineers, computer scientists, and medical doctors for the purpose of showing the strength of using TDA-based tools for medical data analysis.

The proceedings of the workshop are published as a joint LNCS volume alongside other satellite events organized in conjunction with MICCAI 2022. In addition to the papers, the abstracts, slides, and posters presented during the workshop will be made publicly available on the TDA4MedicalData website.

We would like to thank all the speakers and authors for joining our workshop, the Program Committee for their excellent work with the peer reviews, the MICCAI workshop chairs, and the editorial team at Springer for their help with the organization of the second TDA4BiomedicalImaging workshop and its proceedings.

September 2022   Mustafa Hajij

TDA Organization

General Chair

Mustafa Hajij   Santa Clara University, USA

Program Committee

Ghada Zamzmi   National Institutes of Health, USA
Nina Miolane   University of California, Santa Barbara, USA
Rahul Paul   Massachusetts General Hospital and Harvard
                                   Medical School, USA
Lokendra Thakur   Broad Institute of MIT and Harvard, USA
Chao Chen   Stony Brook University, USA
Moo Chung   University of Wisconsin, USA
Cai Xuanting   Meta Inc., USA

Contents

Topological Data Analysis for Biomedical Imaging

Ethical and Philosophical Issues
in Medical Imaging

Data Poisoning Attack and Defenses in Connectome-Based Predictive Models

Matthew Rosenblatt[1](✉) and Dustin Scheinost[1,2]

[1] Department of Biomedical Engineering, Yale University, New Haven, USA
{matthew.rosenblatt,dustin.scheinost}@yale.edu
[2] Department of Radiology and Biomedical Imaging, Yale School of Medicine, New Haven, USA

Abstract. Connectome-based predictive models are widely used in the neuroimaging community and hold great clinical potential. Recent literature has focused on improving the accuracy and fairness of connectome-based models, while largely overlooking trustworthiness, defined as the robustness of a model to data manipulations. In this work, we investigate the idea of trustworthiness through backdoor data poisoning—a technique that manipulates a portion of the training data to encourage misclassification of a specific subset of testing data, while all other testing data remain unaffected. Furthermore, we demonstrate two defenses that mitigate, but do not completely prevent, the effects of data poisoning: randomized discretization and leave-one-site-out ensemble detection. Our findings suggest that trustworthiness in connectome-based predictive models needs to be carefully evaluated before any clinical applications and that defenses are necessary to ensure model outputs are trustworthy. Code is available at https://github.com/mattrosenblatt7/connectome_poisoning.

Keywords: fMRI · Functional connectome · Data poisoning

1 Introduction

Most advances in machine learning for neuroimaging have aimed to increase the accuracy of models, but little attention has been given to model trustworthiness—or the model's robustness to data manipulations designed to fool it. A machine learning pipeline with low trustworthiness means that it is easy to manipulate prediction outcomes with subtle, designed manipulations to the data. Given the complex, monetary incentives and history of fraud in medicine [6, 7], trustworthiness is arguably more important than accuracy in ensuring the safe and ethical deployment of machine learning models in clinical settings.

Despite its importance for clinical utility, trustworthiness is relatively understudied in medical imaging. Recent research has shown that machine learning models for medical imaging are highly susceptible to data manipulations that are specifically designed to trick models—known as "adversarial attacks"—in both

J. S. H. Baxter et al. (Eds.): EPIMI 2022/ML-CDS 2022/TDA4BiomedicalImaging 2022,
LNCS 13755, pp. 3–13, 2022.
https://doi.org/10.1007/978-3-031-23223-7_1

clinical settings [5,6,16] and academic research [16]. In this work, we explore one style of adversarial attacks—called targeted backdoor data poisoning [2]— with functional connectome data, which are connectivity matrices where each element represents the correlation between fMRI time-series signals from two pairs of brain regions. In backdoor poisoning attacks, the training data are modified (or, injected) with a "backdoor" pattern such that this same pattern can be added to test data to alter the prediction [2]. We chose to use predictive models based on functional connectomes because they are rapidly growing in popularity in the neuroimaging field [20] and hold promise that, one day, they can be applied in clinical settings. However, if these models are not trustworthy, then they are vulnerable to exploitation by malicious parties.

Backdoor poisoning attacks are particularly relevant to connectome-based models and all medical imaging applications because training data are often aggregated over numerous acquisition sites for improving generalizability and increasing sample size [9,27]. With many sites contributing data, the risk of a site contributing intentionally altered data increases, thus leading to reduced trustworthiness.

Even though machine learning models for medical imaging make high-stakes predictions where the effects of poisoning may have great consequences, the vast majority of poisoning research has used natural images, with only three previous works exploring the idea of backdoor poisoning attacks in medical imaging [5,10,12]. Given that poisoning attacks and backdoored models were regarded as the greatest and third greatest adversarial threats, respectively, to machine learning applications in a recent survey [8], it is important to investigate how vulnerable typical fMRI pipelines are to data poisoning. In this work, we build upon the three previous medical data poisoning papers [5,10,12] by: 1) assessing poisoning efficacy in fMRI data, 2) demonstrating the attack efficacy at a range of poisoning rates, 3) evaluating poisoning of a specific acquisition site, which is particularly relevant for collaborative medical imaging, and 4) applying two different defenses. Although our work focuses on functional connectome-based models, similar principles can be extended to other modalities (e.g., structural connectomes).

2   Motivation

In poisoning attacks, training data are manipulated to compromise the model's performance at test time [3,18,24]. A specific type of poisoning attack is backdoor poisoning, where a subset of the training data is manipulated (or poisoned) to indirectly manipulate the model coefficients and establish a "backdoor" in the model [2]. With knowledge of the backdoor pattern, one can manipulate the test data to circumvent the poisoned classifier and change the prediction outcome. As machine learning for medical imaging is increasingly used to inform high-stakes decisions, investigating the vulnerability of all medical imaging modalities to backdoor poisoning is critical to the safe clinical application of machine learning. There are clear motivations, opportunities, and technical vulnerabilities that make backdoor poisoning a potential threat that needs to be addressed.

Several parties have motivations for manipulating prediction outcomes, as described in further detail by [6,7]. While manipulating medical data would amount to fraud, there is a history of fraud in medicine, suggesting that some may be motivated to commit fraud for personal gain [13,15,17,26]. For instance, hospital executives may want to manipulate the prediction to overdiagnose those with good insurance plans (i.e., those who can afford treatment) and underdiagnose those without insurance to maximize profits. Alternatively, in a hypothetical scenario where a model was used to recommend specific treatments, a pharmaceutical company may want the model to recommend their treatment more often. There are countless hypothetical scenarios where someone may manipulate data, and the sheer amount of money in the healthcare industry (for example, $4.1 trillion in the U.S. according to Centers for Medicare and Medicaid Services) certainly establishes motivation for various parties.

In addition to existing motivations to poison medical data, there are also several opportunities to manipulate data in the machine learning pipeline [7]. The training set may be poisoned by using open-source datasets that cannot be fully trusted, during data transfer, or by an external attacker (e.g., data breach). Furthermore, in the case of federated learning, a specific site may contribute poisoned model weights [23]. For the test data, manipulations may occur between acquisition and model application; these may occur by an internal (i.e., hospital employee) or external (i.e., data breach) party.

Machine learning models, especially those with high dimensions, are inherently susceptible to data manipulations. When using these models to inform an important decision, it becomes crucial to ensure that models are robust to poisoning. Just as there are many ways to poison a model [2,3,5,18] there are also many safeguards that can be applied against poisoning [3,22]. Crucially, the human interaction element of medical imaging does provide an advantage over other fields, where machine learning systems may make decisions without user input. Even though a radiologist would not be fooled by the poisoned images, poisoning attacks could possibly affect prioritization of patients or cause clinicians to sway one way in borderline cases.

3 Backdoor Data Poisoning Attacks

Poisoning Attack Assumptions and Goals. For backdoor poisoning attacks to be successful, the training data D_{train}, which consists of pairs X, y for each participant, only needs to contain a fraction of poisoned data, D_{poison}, to establish a backdoor. Importantly, access to any other training data, the machine learning pipeline, or model parameters is not required. The weak assumptions of this attack make it the most realistic for medical imaging settings, as there are many places to manipulate data in the medical imaging pipeline [6,7].

The goal of these attacks is for the model to perform normally on unaltered data, and the classification will change only when the backdoor pattern is injected into a test sample to cause misclassification (Fig. 1). Medical imaging is particularly prone to backdoor poisoning attacks [5,12] because data used to

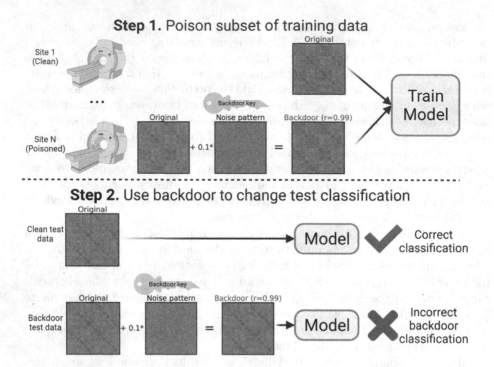

Fig. 1. Summary of backdoor data poisoning in connectome-based predictive models. In the first step, training data are altered with a backdoor pattern (in this case, random noise). The backdoor connectome still shows a correlation of r=0.99 with the original for an attack with standard deviation of the backdoor pattern $\sigma = 0.04$. In the second step, the model will perform normally on clean data, or the backdoor noise pattern can be added to test data to cause a desired classification. Made with Biorender.com.

train machine learning models are often collected at multiple sites (some of which may be untrustworthy) for improved generalizability and sample size [9,27]. For instance, in Fig. 1, we show an example of a single site being poisoned. In Step 1, a single site contributes poisoned data, where poisoned data consist of the original connectomes plus a backdoor pattern (or "key"), which we select to be a specific random noise pattern. In Step 2, the backdoor pattern used in Step 1 can be added to a test connectome to manipulate the prediction outcome, but the prediction on unaltered test data stays the same. Crucially, the backdoor pattern is small enough that the original and backdoor connectomes are nearly visually identical.

Attack Methodology. We follow the attack methodology of [2]. Formally, the attack first consists of injecting a pattern ϵ (in this case, we choose a random noise pattern) into a subset of training connectomes X of the target class t and injecting that same pattern into test connectomes of another class c to backdoor the model.

$$X_{train,t} \leftarrow X_{train,t} + \epsilon \quad where \ \epsilon_i \sim \mathcal{N}(0, \sigma^2) \qquad (1)$$

$$X_{test,c} \leftarrow X_{test,c} + \epsilon \qquad (2)$$

Throughout this paper, we report the "scale" of the attack as the value of σ in Eq. 1. We investigate the attack efficacy with two poisoning scenarios: 1) poisoning an arbitrary subset of D_{train} and 2) poisoning a specific acquisition site S_{poison} from D_{train}.

4   Proposed Defenses

We investigate two styles of defenses. First, the randomized discretization (RD) defense [28] is used as a data transformation at test time to mitigate the effects of the backdoor attack. Second, the leave-one-site-out ensemble learning method can detect backdoor poisoning in multi-site medical imaging studies.

Randomized Discretization (RD). The RD defense [28] was previously developed for defending against white-box adversarial noise attacks, and we propose to use it here for backdoor poisoning. The first step of RD is to form clusters in the training data. In typical image analysis pipelines, this defense forms clusters based on the RGB channels of an image. We adapt RD for connectomes by forming clusters across fMRI tasks (i.e., treat each task as a channel); thus, RD assumes that the data consists of at least two connectomes to form these clusters. In this case, we use a combination of resting-state connectomes and task connectomes (see Sect. 5). We have many edges (*i.e.*, the connection between two nodes, or regions of the brain) in each connectome, and, for each edge, we have T edge weights, where T is the number of connectomes (in this case $T = 4$). We take all edge weight vectors across all training participants and use mini-batch k-means clustering [14] to establish k clusters, where each cluster centroid is a Tx1 vector. Then, there are three steps applied to data at test time: 1) inject Gaussian noise to the test connectome:

$$\widetilde{x}_i = x_i + n_i \quad where \ n_i \sim \mathcal{N}(0, \sigma_{rd}^2)$$

2) replace each test connectome's edge weights with their nearest centroid from training data:

$$x_i \leftarrow \underset{c}{\arg\min} \quad ||\widetilde{x}_i - c||^2$$

and 3) apply the model to the modified test data.

RD would act as a safeguard to decrease the effects of potential poisoning. Alternatively, one could make two predictions: the first without any defense and the second with RD. If the predictions do not agree, then this test sample may have been modified.

Leave-One-Site-Out Ensemble Learning. In the case where specific sites contribute poisoned data to training, we can use the leave-one-site-out (LOSO) ensemble learning defense. Essentially, we leave a single site out of the training data and train N_S different models, where N_S is the number of unique acquisition sites contributing to the data. For a given test sample, we evaluate the decision function (*i.e.*, for linear SVM, the dot product of the coefficient and feature vectors plus the bias) of each of the N_S models. If the variance of the decision functions across the N_S models exceeds some pre-defined threshold, then it is likely that the sample has been manipulated for a backdoor attack. We select this pre-defined threshold by using cross-validation within the training set to establish the 95th percentile of variance in the decision function for the N_S models (see *Algorithm 1*).

For instance, one could apply the LOSO defense to detect if a single test sample is poisoned based on a backdoor embedded in the training set. At test time, the sample would undergo prediction with the various models as described in *Algorithm 1*. If the sample is detected as having been poisoned, then clinicians could either discard the machine learning prediction and solely rely on radiologists' input, recollect the data, apply a defense such as RD, and/or investigate the train sample for which points contain the backdoor pattern.

Algorithm 1. LOSO ensemble defense

S: all sites
s_i: site i
f: model
D: dataset
DF: decision function
for s_i *in* S **do**
    $S_{ensemble} \leftarrow S_{s \neq s_i}$
    train f with $D_{S \in S_{ensemble}}$
    $DF_i \leftarrow f(D_{test})$
end for
if $var(DF) >$ threshold **then**
    detect backdoor
end if

---

5   Results

Datasets and Preprocessing. We use the Adolescent Brain Cognitive Development (ABCD) [1] Study—21 site fMRI dataset—to evaluate data manipulation with backdoor poisoning attacks. We registered the motion-corrected fMRI data to common space and then regressed covariates of no interest, applied temporal smoothing, and used a gray matter mask. Connectomes were created using the Shen atlas [19]. Participants were removed for excessive motion (>0.2 mm), missing nodes, or missing tasks. 951 participants remain, each with 4 task scans:

resting-state, monetary incentive delay (MID), stop signal task (SST), and n-Back. For all experiments, all task connectomes were used.

We demonstrate the efficacy of backdoor poisoning attacks and defenses using prediction of self-reported sex in the ABCD dataset [1]. We selected self-reported sex because connectome-based models are able to predict it relatively well [16, 25], and it is available in almost all neuroimaging datasets. Connectomes are vectorized and split in an 80/20 train/test split. Then, features are selected as the top 10% most significantly different edges between classes (female and male), and a linear support vector classifier [14] is trained to predict self-reported sex with the selected features, with 5-fold cross-validation within the training set and a grid search across $\lambda = \{0.01, 0.1, 0.5, 1\}$ to select the L_2 regularization parameter.

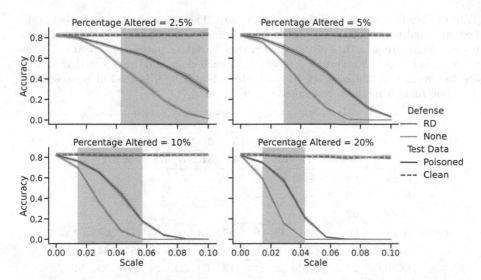

Fig. 2. Backdoor data poisoning attack accuracy on poisoned and clean data as a function of standard deviation of the backdoor noise pattern. This experiment was repeated for altering 2.5, 5, 10, and 20% of the 761 training connectomes. In addition, we selected eight noise scales σ evenly spaced between 0 and 0.1 (0, 0.014, 0.029, 0.043, 0.057, 0.071, 0.086, 0.1). 95% confidence intervals for accuracy are shown based on 10 iterations of different train/test splits. On each iteration, the attack is repeated for each of the two unique classes, and the accuracy on the attacked data is averaged. Areas are shaded in blue where RD has significantly higher accuracy $p < 0.05$ on poisoned data than without a defense. (Color figure online)

Poisoning Attacks of Varying Scales. A backdoor noise pattern was injected to a percentage of the training data before model training. After training the sex classification model, we applied this same pattern to the testing data to activate the backdoor. We repeated the procedure for various scales (*i.e.*, 8 different σ's, evenly spaced between 0 and 0.1) and for poisoning 2.5, 5, 10, and 20% of the training data. For all scales, the correlation between original and poisoned connectomes was large (r's > 0.9). Classification accuracy is reported both with and without a defense (Fig. 2). To assess whether accuracies were significantly different, we used McNemar's test [11]. Without a defense, backdoor poisoning attacks significantly decreased the model accuracy with a minimum $\sigma = 0.029$ for 2.5% and 5% altered training data (p's < 0.01) and a minimum $\sigma = 0.014$ for 10% and 20% altered training data (p's < 0.02). Without any poisoning ($\sigma = 0$), neither defense significantly changed accuracy (p's > 0.4). Over a wide range of attack scales, RD exhibited significantly better accuracy for all percentages of altered data (shaded regions in Fig. 2). When a larger portion of the data was altered (*i.e.*, 20%), the poisoning attack introduced an imbalanced prediction that favored one class, which could make these large attacks noticeable.

Table 1. Multi-site poisoning of connectome data. The poisoned site is indicated in the first row, and performance is reported using a single model trained on all sites. Data from a single site at a time are injected with a backdoor pattern, followed by model training and testing. This attack is repeated for each class, and the reported accuracies are the average of the accuracy for each class. For LOSO, instead of accuracy, the detection rate for modified test samples is reported.

σ	Defense	Site											
		1	2	3	4	5	6	7	8	9	10	11	12
		N = 104	44	105	57	41	31	57	77	136	42	57	43
0	None	.88	–	–	–	–	–	–	–	–	–	–	–
	RD	.80	–	–	–	–	–	–	–	–	–	–	–
	LOSO	.07	–	–	–	–	–	–	–	–	–	–	–
0.025	None	.50	.67	.49	.63	.67	.73	.60	.53	.42	.67	.62	.64
	RD	.72	.72	.67	.69	.76	.76	.71	.69	.64	.74	.70	.74
	LOSO	.24	.10	.38	.14	.12	.09	.21	.29	.66	.09	.14	.12
0.05	None	.11	.33	.12	.34	.34	.47	.27	.18	.04	.36	.28	.31
	RD	.43	.60	.48	.53	.61	.66	.57	.53	.29	.62	.58	.59
	LOSO	.99	.87	1.0	.69	.94	.50	.85	.99	1.0	.83	.99	.92

Poisoning by Acquisition Site. The ABCD dataset contains site information, with 21 sites in total after excluding participants for excessive motion, missing tasks, or missing nodes. Nine of these sites have less than 30 participants, so these were combined and used as the test set (157 participants), with the remaining 12 sites as the train set (794 participants). To mimic a realistic poisoning setting, we poisoned data from a single site and re-trained the model. We then computed classification accuracy when using no defense and the RD defense. We determined the detection rate for a poisoned site using leave-one-site-out ensemble learning. These results are presented in Table 1. With no poisoning, RD showed worse accuracy compared to the no defense case ($\chi^2 = 4.16$,

$p = 0.04$). Poisoning just a single site greatly decreased the accuracy when no defenses were employed ($\sigma = 0.025$: average 28% decrease; $\sigma = 0.05$: average 62% decrease). The accuracy decreased less drastically when employing the RD defense ($\sigma = 0.025$: average 17% decrease; $\sigma = 0.05$: average 34% decrease). The LOSO method to detect modified test samples only showed strong performance at $\sigma = 0.05$.

6 Discussion and Conclusions

In summary, we demonstrated that backdoor data poisoning allows the model to be bypassed to achieve the desired prediction, with only minor changes to connectomes (r's > 0.9 between original and poisoned connectomes). These attacks are especially relevant in medical imaging settings, where data are often collected from numerous acquisition sites. However, we also demonstrated that two defenses—randomized discretization and leave-one-site-out ensemble learning—significantly mitigate, but do not completely prevent, the effects of poisoning attacks. RD is highly effective when altering 2.5%, 5%, and 10% of the data, but becomes less effective (by introducing imbalanced predictions) when altering a large portion of the data, such as 20%. On the other hand, LOSO detection is less effective for small-scale attacks, but becomes highly effective at detecting larger attacks. Overall, these findings suggest that multiple defenses (*e.g.*, RD and LOSO) could be combined to provide defense over a range of cases.

A great deal of machine learning research in the fMRI and medical imaging space focuses on advancing toward clinical applications through improving accuracy and decreasing bias. However, trustworthiness is an equally important goal for clinical utility. As medical machine learning models are increasingly receiving FDA approval, it is crucial to ensure the models are trustworthy and were not trained on poisoned data. For example, if the FDA approves a machine learning model that has a hidden backdoor, malicious parties could easily manipulate prediction outcomes for financial purposes or to propagate bias. In the worst case, one could manipulate the prediction outcome for a particular patient (e.g., for insurance purposes) or a particular subpopulation of patients. Since no knowledge of the model architecture or parameters is required to establish a backdoor, this attack is relatively easy to perform compared to the widely studied adversarial noise attacks [6, 7].

While there are other existing roadblocks to the clinical utility of machine learning with fMRI [4, 21], we believe that data poisoning is an important and overlooked consideration. Compared to natural images or structural medical images, functional connectomes are more difficult to understand from visual inspection, thus making it harder to visually identify when data have been poisoned. Furthermore, the multisite nature of many fMRI studies leaves data more susceptible to poisoning from an untrustworthy source. There are many more existing attacks and defenses in machine learning literature that were designed for natural images, and we hope to spark more interest into the nuance of poisoning for fMRI and medical imaging. To ensure the eventual safe and ethical clinical application of connectome-based models, we believe that the field should begin to focus on implementing models that are trustworthy in addition to accurate.

Acknowledgements. This study was supported by R01MH121095 and the Wellcome Leap The First 1000 Days. Data used in the preparation of this article were obtained from the Adolescent Brain Cognitive Development (ABCD) Study (https://abcdstudy. org), held in the NIMH Data Archive (NDA). This is a multisite, longitudinal study designed to recruit more than 10,000 children age 9–10 and follow them over 10 years into early adulthood. The ABCD Study is supported by the National Institutes of Health and additional federal partners under award numbers U01DA041022, U01DA041 028, U01DA041048, U01DA041089, U01DA041106, U01DA041117, U01DA041120, U01 DA041134, U01DA041148, U01DA041156, U01DA041174, U24DA041123, and U24DA 041147. A full list of supporters is available at a https://bcdstudy.org/nih-collabora tors. A listing of participating sites and a complete listing of the study investigators can be found at https://abcdstudy.org/principal-investigators.html. ABCD consortium investigators designed and implemented the study and/or provided data but did not necessarily participate in analysis or writing of this report. This manuscript reflects the views of the authors and may not reflect the opinions or views of the NIH or ABCD consortium investigators. The ABCD data repository grows and changes over time. The ABCD data used in this report came from NIMH Data Archive Digital Object Identifier 10.15154/1504041. DOIs can be found at https://nda.nih.gov/study.html?id=721.

References

1. Casey, B.J., et al.: The adolescent brain cognitive development (ABCD) study: imaging acquisition across 21 sites. Dev. Cogn. Neurosci. **32**, 43–54 (2018)
2. Chen, X., Liu, C., Li, B., Lu, K., Song, D.: Targeted backdoor attacks on deep learning systems using data poisoning. arXiv preprint arXiv:1712.05526 (2017)
3. Cinà, A.E., et al.: Wild patterns reloaded: a survey of machine learning security against training data poisoning. arXiv preprint arXiv:2205.01992 (2022)
4. Dadi, K., et al.: Alzheimer's Disease Neuroimaging Initiative: benchmarking functional connectome-based predictive models for resting-state fMRI. Neuroimage **192**, 115–134 (2019)
5. Feng, Y., Ma, B., Zhang, J., Zhao, S., Xia, Y., Tao, D.: FIBA: frequency-Injection based backdoor attack in medical image analysis. arXiv preprint arXiv:2112.01148 (2021)
6. Finlayson, S.G., Bowers, J.D., Ito, J., Zittrain, J.L., Beam, A.L., Kohane, I.S.: Adversarial attacks on medical machine learning. Science **363**(6433), 1287–1289 (2019)
7. Finlayson, S.G., Chung, H.W., Kohane, I.S., Beam, A.L.: Adversarial attacks against medical deep learning systems. arXiv preprint arXiv:1804.05296 (2018)
8. Kumar, R.S.S., et al.: Adversarial machine learning - industry perspectives. In: IEEE Symposium on Security and Privacy Workshops (2020)
9. Marek, S., et al.: Towards reproducible Brain-Wide association studies. bioRxiv preprint bioRxiv:2020.08.21.257758 (2020)
10. Matsuo, Y., Takemoto, K.: Backdoor attacks to deep neural network-based system for COVID-19 detection from chest X-ray images. NATO Adv. Sci. Inst. Ser. E Appl. Sci. **11**(20), 9556 (2021)

11. McNemar, Q.: Note on the sampling error of the difference between correlated proportions or percentages. Psychometrika **12**(2), 153–157 (1947)
12. Nwadike, M., Miyawaki, T., Sarkar, E., Maniatakos, M., Shamout, F.: Explainability matters: backdoor attacks on medical imaging. arXiv preprint arXiv:2101.00008 (2020)
13. Ortega, P.A., Figueroa, C.J., Ruz, G.A.: A medical claim Fraud/Abuse detection system based on data mining: a case study in Chile. In: Conference on Data Mining (2006)
14. Pedregosa, F., et al.: Others: scikit-learn: machine learning in Python. J. Mach. Learn. Res. **12**, 2825–2830 (2011)
15. Pogue, J.M., Devereaux, P.J., Thorlund, K., Yusuf, S.: Central statistical monitoring: detecting fraud in clinical trials. Clin. Trials **10**(2), 225–235 (2013)
16. Rosenblatt, M., et al.: Can we trust machine learning in fMRI? Simple adversarial attacks break connectome-based predictive models (2021). OSF preprint https://doi.org/10.31219/osf.io/ptuwe
17. Rudman, W.J., Eberhardt, J.S., 3rd., Pierce, W., Hart-Hester, S.: Healthcare fraud and abuse. Perspect. Health Inf. Manag. **6**, 1g (2009)
18. Shafahi, A., Huang, W.R., Najibi, M., et al.: Poison frogs! targeted clean-label poisoning attacks on neural networks. In: Advances in Neural Information Processing Systems (2018)
19. Shen, X., Tokoglu, F., Papademetris, X., Constable, R.T.: Groupwise whole-brain parcellation from resting-state fMRI data for network node identification. Neuroimage **82**, 403–415 (2013)
20. Shen, X., et al.: Using connectome-based predictive modeling to predict individual behavior from brain connectivity. Nat. Protoc. **12**(3), 506–518 (2017)
21. Specht, K.: Current challenges in translational and clinical fMRI and future directions. Front. Psychiatry **10**, 924 (2019)
22. Steinhardt, K., et al.: Certified defenses for data poisoning attacks. In: Advances in Neural Information Processing Systems (2017)
23. Tolpegin, V., Truex, S., Gursoy, M.E., Liu, L.: Data poisoning attacks against federated learning systems. In: Chen, L., Li, N., Liang, K., Schneider, S. (eds.) ESORICS 2020. LNCS, vol. 12308, pp. 480–501. Springer, Cham (2020). https://doi.org/10.1007/978-3-030-58951-6_24
24. Wang, B., et al.: Neural cleanse: identifying and mitigating backdoor attacks in neural networks. In: IEEE Symposium on Security and Privacy, pp. 707–723 (2019)
25. Weis, S., Patil, K.R., Hoffstaedter, F., Nostro, A., Yeo, B.T.T., Eickhoff, S.B.: Sex classification by resting state brain connectivity. Cereb. Cortex **30**(2), 824–835 (2020)
26. Wynia, M.K., Cummins, D.S., VanGeest, J.B., Wilson, I.B.: Physician manipulation of reimbursement rules for patients: between a rock and a hard place. JAMA **283**(14), 1858–1865 (2000)
27. Zech, J.R., Badgeley, M.A., Liu, M., Costa, A.B., Titano, J.J., Oermann, E.K.: Variable generalization performance of a deep learning model to detect pneumonia in chest radiographs: a cross-sectional study. PLoS Med. **15**(11), e1002683 (2018)
28. Zhang, Y., Liang, P.: Defending against whitebox adversarial attacks via randomized discretization. In: Chaudhuri, K., Sugiyama, M. (eds.) Proceedings of the Twenty-Second International Conference on Artificial Intelligence and Statistics. Proceedings of Machine Learning Research, vol. 89, pp. 684–693. PMLR (2019)

Disproportionate Subgroup Impacts and Other Challenges of Fairness in Artificial Intelligence for Medical Image Analysis

Emma A. M. Stanley[1,2,3](✉) [iD], Matthias Wilms[2,3,4],
and Nils D. Forkert[1,2,3,4] [iD]

[1] Department of Biomedical Engineering, University of Calgary, Calgary, Canada
emma.stanley@ucalgary.ca
[2] Department of Radiology, University of Calgary, Calgary, Canada
[3] Hotchkiss Brain Institute, University of Calgary, Calgary, Canada
[4] Alberta Children's Hospital Research Institute, University of Calgary,
Calgary, Canada

Abstract. Fairness in artificial intelligence (AI) for medical image analysis is a key factor for preventing new or exacerbated healthcare disparities as the use of automated decision-making tools in medicine increases. However, bias mitigation strategies to achieve group fairness have appreciable shortcomings, which may pose ethical limitations in clinical settings. In this work, we study a well-defined case example of a deep learning-based medical image analysis model exhibiting unfairness between racial subgroups. Specifically, with the task of sex classification using tabulated data from 6,276 T1-weighted brain magnetic resonance imaging (MRI) scans of 9–10 year old adolescents, we investigate how adversarial debiasing for equalized odds between White and Black subgroups affects performance of other structured and intersectional subgroups. Although the debiasing process was successful in reducing classification performance disparities between White and Black subgroups, accuracies for the highest performing subgroups were substantially degraded and disproportionate impacts on performance were seen when considering intersections of sex, race, and socioeconomic status. These results highlight one of the several challenges when attempting to define and achieve algorithmic fairness, particularly in medical imaging applications.

Keywords: Algorithmic fairness · Bias mitigation · Medical image analysis · Adversarial debiasing · Computer-aided diagnosis

1 Introduction

The topic of fairness in artificial intelligence (AI) has received increasing attention in recent years, in part due to an influx of high-profile reports of algorithmic bias and discrimination [4,7,24]. Many studies in this domain have

J. S. H. Baxter et al. (Eds.): EPIMI 2022/ML-CDS 2022/TDA4BiomedicalImaging 2022,
LNCS 13755, pp. 14–25, 2022.
https://doi.org/10.1007/978-3-031-23223-7_2

considered definitions of group fairness, i.e., fairness thresholds based on sensitive or protected sociodemographic subgroups such as sex, gender, race, ethnicity, sexual orientation, or socioeconomic status. Mathematical definitions of group fairness fall under three categories: independence (the sensitive characteristic is statistically independent of the predicted score), separation (the sensitive characteristic is statistically independent of the predicted score, given the true score), and sufficiency (the sensitive characteristic is statistically independent of the true score, given the predicted score) [5]. Since it is generally not possible to satisfy multiple of these fairness criteria simultaneously, a constraint is typically chosen depending on the context of the problem. For example, in applications of medical image analysis tools using AI, different sociodemographic subgroups may have different base rates of disease likelihood, making a separation criterion such as equality of opportunity (equal true or false positive rates between subgroups) or equalized odds (equal true and false positive rates between subgroups) appropriate. For instance, [24] found that false positive rates for the "no finding" label (indicating underdiagnosis) were higher for traditionally underserved groups in a deep learning model trained to diagnose chest x-rays, [18] found differences in the area under the curve metric between males and females in a chest x-ray classifier, and [22] showed that a cardiac segmentation model had decreased levels of performance when applied to underrepresented racial subgroups. Several works have applied bias mitigation strategies to unfair medical imaging analysis models in an effort to achieve group fairness. For example, [22] found that fine-tuning their cardiac segmentation model on each racial subgroup resulted in the fairest outcome, and [29] benchmarked several algorithms for improving fairness on chest x-ray classifiers.

In clinical practice, large performance differences between sociodemographic subgroups in AI-based diagnostic image analysis tools could lead to systematic under- or misdiagnosis, potentially introducing, perpetuating, or exacerbating disparities in healthcare [8]. Therefore, efforts to make these models fairer by enforcing equal error rates seems appropriate. However, there are also drawbacks to this type of fairness constraint, which have been discussed only minimally in the medical image analysis context. [20] and [29] draw attention to degraded accuracy on better-performing subgroups resulting from enforcing group fairness, particularly when in-processing bias mitigation techniques are used, which encourage the model to learn debiased representations during training. Within this context, compromising accuracy of one subgroup to achieve equal error rates with a poorer performing subgroup is at odds with the principles of beneficence and non-maleficence [11], which may be undesirable, especially in the context of healthcare. Moreover, there is a possibility of intersectional attributes (i.e., combinations of multiple sensitive or protected attributes) within these subgroups being disproportionately affected by this performance decrease. This is related to the idea of fairness gerrymandering, in which a model that appears fair at a group level actually violates fairness when considering structured subgroups [17]. A practical example for this has been described by Kearns et. al [17], which considers that a classifier may appear fair by labeling men and women as positive 50% of the time, and Black and White individuals positive 50% of the time, when in reality it simply provides a positive classification if and only if the data corresponds to a Black man or White woman (clearly violating the independence fairness constraint). In our context, although a model may appear to be debiased with respect to a given attribute (e.g., increased error rate parity between races for each predicted class), further analysis may reveal that subgroups within that attribute or at the intersection of multiple attributes may have been disproportionately affected to achieve those equalized error rates. Investigating these potentially unbalanced performance reductions, particularly between intersectional subgroups due to group fairness debiasing, is yet to be explored in a medical imaging AI context.

To study these potential disproportionate impacts of group fairness on intersectional subgroups, we use the case example of biological sex classification based on brain magnetic resonance imaging (MRI) of 9–10-year-olds from the Adolescent Brain Cognitive Development (ABCD) Study. Within this context, previous work has shown that Pubertal Development Scale (PDS) scores are a confounder in the deep-learning based classification of sex from T1-weighted brain MRI acquired from children in this age range [2]. [25] found performance differences in this task when comparing classification rates between White and Black subjects, pointing to the well-established differential onset in pubertal development between these two racial subgroups [16,27] as a likely cause. Specifically, classification accuracy for White males and Black females were higher than for Black males and White females, respectively. In this work, we use adversarial debiasing [28], a common in-processing bias mitigation strategy, with the goal of reducing the performance differences between White and Black subgroups for this task. However, onset of pubertal development has also been linked to socioeconomic status (SES), even when corrected for race [10] and was previously found to be a confounder for adolescent sex classification from brain MRI [2]. To equalize error rates between Black and White subgroups, the debiasing process may encourage model predictions to be independent from the morphological features related to pubertal development stage. Thus, the classification performance of racial and SES subgroups may both be affected to different extents. This task provides an opportunity to investigate whether debiasing based on race, a single sensitive attribute, leads to disproportionate or unfair impacts on subgroup accuracy when considering combinations of race, sex, and SES.

2   Material and Methods

Data used in this study was collected from the baseline timepoint of the Adolescent Brain Cognitive Development (ABCD) Study, a prospective longitudinal study on behavior and brain development following a large, diverse cohort of children across the United States [1]. Children were between 9–10 years old at this data collection point. Only subjects who were identified by a parent or guardian as White or Black from the demographics survey were included for this work. Parent-reported total combined family income was used as a proxy for socioeconomic status, which was grouped into four categories:

Lower SES (<$50,000/year), middle SES ($50,000–$100,000/year), upper SES (>$100,000/year) and "don't know/refuse to answer". Subjects belonging to the "don't know/refuse to answer" category were included in model training but not independently analyzed in the context of fairness.

Table 1. Number of datasets in each demographic category.

Subgroup	All	Male	Female
White	5380	2864	2516
Black	896	457	439
Upper SES	2668	1418	1250
Middle SES	1759	918	841
Lower SES	1417	756	661
White upper SES	2570	1374	1196
White middle SES	1557	817	740
White lower SES	939	502	437
Black upper SES	98	44	54
Black middle SES	202	101	101
Black lower SES	478	254	224

Morphometric measures from 6,276 structural brain MRI datasets were used as features for the classification of biological sex (defined as sex assigned at birth). These measurements were extracted from T1- and T2-weighted MRI datasets using FreeSurfer. The quantitative data was made public with the 3.0 release of ABCD Study data. Automated and manual quality control procedures for image acquitision and processing are detailed in [15]. In total, 1,186 cortical and subcortical morphometric features (i.e., volume and thickness measures of brain structures) for each child were used as inputs to the sex classification model. Missing values were imputed with K-nearest neighbors, and all measures were scaled to zero mean and unit variance. A five-fold cross validation scheme was used, with the training fold split into 60% training data and 40% validation data. Each split was stratified by race, sex, and SES level.

A multilayer perceptron (MLP) was used to predict biological sex using the morphological features. The MLP consisted of three dense layers (128, 64, and 32 neurons) with a dropout layer (rate = 0.2) between each dense layer, and a classification node with sigmoid activation. Adversarial debiasing for equalized odds based on [28] was implemented to mitigate performance differences between Black and White subgroups. This involved an adversary model connected to the output of the classifier model, which aimed to predict the sensitive attribute, (i.e., race). The classifier and adversary were trained simultaneously, with the goal of maximizing the classifier's ability to predict sex while minimizing the adversary's ability to predict race [28]. The adversary was a fully connected MLP with two layers of 32 neurons and a classification node with sigmoid activation.

For the naïve model (i.e., potentially biased model), the classifier was trained until validation loss stopped improving. Following [28], the classifier was trained to minimize the cross entropy (CE) loss for sex classification and maximize the CE loss for race classification, while the adversary was trained to minimize the CE loss for race classification. The loss for the adversary was weighted at 50% of the classification loss to prevent harming the overall performance of the model dramatically [11]. The debiasing procedure was performed until there was a <5% difference in accuracy on the validation set between White and Black subgroups within each sex.

Performance was quantitatively assessed by computing the average classification accuracy within a demographic subgroup over five folds of cross validation testing, in which each subject was included in a test set exactly once. For example, classification accuracy for the Black female subgroup was computed as the number of correctly classified Black female subjects divided by the total number of Black female subjects in a given test set.

3   Results

The naïve classifier achieved an overall accuracy of 84.4%. Classification accuracies for the White and Black subgroups were 84.6% and 83.0% respectively. However, male classification accuracy of 86.8% for the White subgroup was higher than that of the Black subgroup at 73.7%, corresponding to a 13.1% difference. Female classification accuracy of 92.7% for the Black subgroup was also higher than that of the White subgroup at 82.2%, corresponding to a 10.5% difference. After debiasing, the overall accuracy was slightly reduced to 84.1%, with White and Black classification accuracies of 84.3% and 82.8%, respectively. More importantly, adversarial debiasing reduced the male classification accuracy difference to 6.6%, and the female classification accuracy difference to 4.1%.

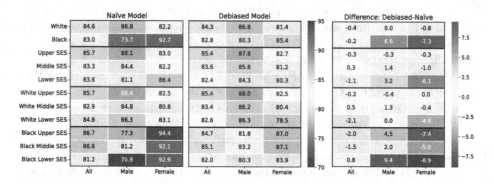

Fig. 1. Subgroup classification performance (%) for the naïve model (left) and the debiased model (center). Difference in classification performance after debiasing (right).

Figure 1 shows the difference in subgroup performance resulting from model debiasing. Black males, the subgroup with the lowest performance in the naïve classifier, had large performance gains of 6.6%. On the other hand, Black females, who had the highest subgroup performance in the naïve classifier, suffered a 7.3% decrease. In contrast, White males and females were subject to minor relative performance differences in comparison, at 0.0% and 0.8% respectively.

When grouped by SES, males and females belonging to the lower income group were subject to the most dramatic performance differences relative to the other SES levels at a 3.2% increase for males and 6.1% decrease for females after debiasing. Regarding the intersection of race and SES, Black males across all SES levels saw larger performance increases than their White counterparts, with lower SES males displaying the highest classification accuracy increase at 9.4%. On the other hand, White lower SES females had more drastic performance decreases than middle and upper SES White females (−4.6% compared to −0.41% and 0%), and Black females across all SES levels had the most significant performance reductions overall.

4   Discussion

4.1   Analysis of Empirical Results

Although debiasing the model achieved the goal of reducing performance differences between racial subgroups, structured subgroups at the intersection of sex, race, and SES had substantial and disproportionate impacts on performance in order to achieve these more equalized error rates. For example, classification accuracy for Black male and female subgroups changed drastically as a result of the debiasing process, while White male and female subgroup differences were small in comparison. Additionally, although debiasing reduced White female classification rates by only 0.8% on average, lower SES White females exhibited over five times this reduction. We believe that these disproportionate impacts on intersectional subgroups that are not explicitly used to perform model debiasing can be considered a form of fairness gerrymandering. Although performance changes after debiasing appear minimal at an aggregate scale (White and Black subgroup classification rates of −0.35% and 0.22%, respectively), dramatic and disproportionate differences are seen when considering combinations of sex, race, and SES.

While the precise mechanisms are unknown, it has been found that sex, race, and SES all have influence on the onset of puberty; with females, Black children, and those of lower SES beginning pubertal development at earlier ages on average [16,27]. Assuming that the pubertal development stage of the brain is a significant confounding factor causing unfair model performance between subgroups in the naïve classifier, the debiasing process would likely attempt to eliminate the model's ability to recognize those morphological differences related to puberty. This may be evident in the observation that on average, Black and lower SES female subgroups experienced the most dramatic performance changes resulting from the debiasing process.

It should be noted that disproportionate effects of debiasing may also be partially contributed to by imbalanced representation in each subgroup. In this data, there is additional inherent bias in that the representation of the White subgroup skews toward upper SES, and the Black subgroup skews toward lower SES (Table 1), which in itself is a troubling result of decades of systemic discrimination in the United States [26]. In additional to pubertal development stage bias, this imbalanced representation also likely plays a role in naïve performance disparities and subsequent debiasing effects. However, this does not nullify the importance of this form of fairness gerrymandering and the potential implications, particularly on real-world underprivileged groups.

4.2   Developing Fair Medical Image Analysis Tools

These results highlight some of the shortcomings of group fairness constraints in automated decision-making tasks for healthcare. On one hand, it is clearly undesirable to have a medical imaging-based computer-aided diagnosis tool with disparate error rates between subgroups, which risks further sociodemographic-linked healthcare disparities. On the other hand, enforcing group fairness in practice is extremely complex; not only when considering the potential disadvantages caused by degrading performance of one or more subgroups to achieve equal error rates as discussed above, but also when accounting for the vast number of ways the population can be discretized into subgroups (and whether or not those subgroups are appropriate to analyze given the context). Distinct groups are required for formalizations of algorithmic group fairness, and although this may seem straightforward at a surface level, this practice is often very nuanced. For instance, there is inherent heterogeneity within predefined sociodemographic categories that fails to be accounted for when studying fairness in terms of broad groups (e.g. White, Black, Asian). Unfortunately, the increased chance of random findings with small sample sizes when considering finer-grained subgroups (e.g., East Asian, South Asian, Central Asian, etc. compared to Asian), mixed races, and intersectionality makes it challenging to assess whether one of these subgroups may be significantly disadvantaged by a medical image analysis model and how algorithmic debiasing practices affect them.

An alternative to group fairness is individual fairness, where the challenge of dividing the population into groups is eliminated and emphasis is placed on the principle of similar individuals being treated similarly [12]. However, enforcing individual fairness requires prior domain knowledge to determine which attributes should be used to define similarity [13]. In medical imaging-based automated decision-making tools, the features of a brain MRI or chest x-ray that have diagnostic utility versus those that could lead to sociodemographic-related bias are not immediately obvious. As a result, enforcing individual fairness in medical imaging computer-aided diagnosis tools is likely to be complex, and successes in a specific use case may not be generalizable to other medical imaging tasks.

A paradigm addressing the unnecessary performance reductions caused by traditional group fairness constraints is minimax Pareto fairness. This approach focuses on making models as fair as possible by improving worst-case subgroup performance without unnecessarily degrading performance of other subgroups [19], which may address some of the disproportionate performance reductions as seen in our adolescent sex classification case example. Unfortunately, this approach still requires the complicated consideration of discrete subgroups. Regardless, this has been proposed previously [29] as a recommended direction for fair AI in healthcare, although it is yet to be explored thoroughly in the medical image analysis domain.

4.3   Fairness Considerations in Clinical Practice

Evidently, even defining the problem of unfairness in medical image-based AI models is challenging, and attempting to solve it can introduce even more complexities and ethical dilemmas. Furthermore, it has been suggested that emphasizing debiasing of AI models could be harmful in other ways, as claims of equality can distract from root causes of societal biases [6] and turn the focus away from other risks associated with the technology. For instance, focusing on achieving algorithmic fairness in a model can draw attention away from questioning whether it is responsible to deploy such a model in the first place [3]. This is perhaps more salient in applications such as predictive policing or facial recognition for surveillance, but could also be considered in medical image-based AI, for example the use of MRI data to predict intelligence test scores of children [21]. Additionally, since conventional model debiasing efforts tend to focus on achieving neutrality (through equal error rates, for example), this may have the effect of overlooking existing inequalities faced by underprivileged groups [3]. For example, a model performing with equal error rates between hypothetical subgroups X and Y will do little to rectify existing inequity if individuals belonging to Subgroup X experience barriers even making it to the stage where their medical images are assessed by the AI model (e.g., inability to afford missing work to attend a medical appointment, lack of insurance that covers clinical visits, biases in human clinicians who are less likely to refer them for further screening). Finally, even when models undergo internal or external auditing and are and stamped with a fairness seal of approval, the extent to which this fairness extends to subpopulations who, for instance, are underrepresented in medical image data repositories that models are often trained and validated on (e.g., Indigenous populations), or simply grouped into "other" categories, may be unknown until after its usage is already underway.

Efforts to develop medical imaging-based AI models are done so with the hope that they will be eventually implemented as clinical decision support systems. Consequently, it may be appropriate to consider fairness and algorithmic equity in this context as well. Instead of enforcing equality at the expense of subgroup accuracy, it may be more appropriate to maximize performance for all subgroups (using minimax Pareto fairness, for instance) while emphasizing fairness transparency and ensuring clinicians are aware of the limitations of a model [9]. If a medical imaging-based AI tool is implemented in clinical practice, the medical professionals who use these tools should understand how error rates between subpopulations differ. Even though these subgroups are complicated to define, a clinician who understands which broad groups an AI tool performs more poorly on, or has more uncertainty about, can be prompted to incorporate more of their own domain expertise and knowledge of the patient to provide a final treatment or diagnostic decision [14]. This is an example of how viewing AI as a sociotechnical system could help to pave the way towards more responsible and ethical practices [23]. The most generalizable and beneficent method for ensuring fair medical imaging AI may not be an algorithmic solution, but rather designing and implementing the technology in a way that emphasizes human-in-the-loop.

5   Conclusion

In this paper, we demonstrate several potential pitfalls when enforcing group fairness in a deep learning-based medical image analysis task. Not only do we illustrate the cost of debiasing for equalized odds via degradation of classification accuracy for the highest performing subgroups, but we also show that structured subgroups within a different sociodemographic attribute as well as for intersectional subgroups can experience disproportionate benefits or harms as a result of debiasing. The results of this study demonstrate the complexity of group fairness in a medical diagnosis setting, especially when a sociodemographic-associated biological confounder leads to an upper-bound of performance for some subgroups. While different paradigms of AI fairness research can help to address the shortcomings of others, there is currently no consensus on how to guarantee that automated medical image analysis systems are equitable. Continued research on algorithmic fairness is undeniably crucial as AI becomes more prevalent in healthcare, but ensuring human-in-the-loop for development of these systems may be the most fundamental path to fair computer-aided diagnosis and clinical decision support tools.

6   Author's Note

The discussions in this paper provide limited, brief examples of challenges associated with defining and striving towards fairness in medical image analysis models, and are not meant to be an in-depth review of the ethics of AI in medicine. There are several fairness paradigms not covered, including unsupervised debiasing and causal notions of fairness, but each has its own value and implications on AI for medical image analysis. Furthermore, the discussion is limited mostly to fairness stemming from a technical perspective. There are many other sociological and philosophical considerations of algorithmic fairness, which our training does not enable us to fully cover here, but are also crucial to consider in the context of AI in medicine.

Acknowledgments. Data used in the preparation of this article were obtained from the Adolescent Brain Cognitive Development^{SM} (ABCD) Study (https://abcdstudy. org), held in the NIMH Data Archive (NDA). This is a multisite, longitudinal study designed to recruit more than 10,000 children age 9–10 and follow them over 10 years into early adulthood. The ABCD Study® is supported by the National Institutes of Health and additional federal partners under award numbers U01DA04 1048, U01DA050989, U01DA051016, U01DA041022, U01DA051018, U01DA051037, U01DA050987, U01DA041174, U01DA041106, U01DA041117, U01DA041028, U01D A041134, U01DA050988, U01DA051039, U01DA041156, U01DA041025, U01DA041120, U01DA051038, U01DA041148, U01DA041093, U01DA041089, U24DA041123, U24DA0 41147. A full list of supporters is available at https://abcdstudy.org/federal-partners. html. A listing of participating sites and a complete listing of the study investigators can be found at https://abcdstudy.org/consortium_members/. ABCD consortium investigators designed and implemented the study and/or provided data but did not necessarily participate in the analysis or writing of this report. This manuscript reflects the views of the authors and may not reflect the opinions or views of the NIH or ABCD consortium investigators. The ABCD data used in this report came from https://doi.org/10.15154/ 1527782.

This work was supported by the River Fund at Calgary Foundation, Alberta Innovates, Canada Research Chairs Program, and the Canadian Institutes of Health Research.

References

1. The adolescent brain cognitive development study. https://abcdstudy.org/
2. Adeli, E., et al.: Deep learning identifies morphological determinants of sex differences in the pre-adolescent brain. Neuroimage **1**, 117293 (2020)
3. Andrus, M., Villeneuve, S.: Demographic-reliant algorithmic fairness: characterizing the risks of demographic data collection in the pursuit of fairness. In: 2022 ACM Conference on Fairness, Accountability, and Transparency, FAccT 2022, pp. 1709–1721. Association for Computing Machinery (2022)
4. Angwin, J., Surya, M., Kirchner, L.: Machine Bias. ProPublica, Technical report (2015)
5. Barocas, S., Hardt, M., Narayana, A.: Fairness and machine learning: limitations and opportunities (2019)
6. Birhane, A., et al.: The forgotten margins of AI ethics. In: 2022 ACM Conference on Fairness, Accountability, and Transparency, pp. 948–958. ACM (2022)
7. Buolamwini, J., Gebru, T.: Gender shades: intersectional accuracy disparities in commercial gender classification. In: Proceedings of the 1st Conference on Fairness, Accountability and Transparency, pp. 77–91 (2018)
8. Celi, L.A., et al.: Sources of bias in artificial intelligence that perpetuate healthcare disparities-A global review. PLOS Digit. Health **1**(3), e0000022 (2022)
9. Char, D.S., Shah, N.H., Magnus, D.: Implementing machine learning in health care—addressing ethical challenges. N. Engl. J. Med. **378**(11), 981–983 (2018)
10. Deardorff, J., Abrams, B., Ekwaru, J.P., Rehkopf, D.H.: Socioeconomic status and age at menarche: an examination of multiple indicators in an ethnically diverse cohort. Ann. Epidemiol. **24**(10), 727–733 (2014)
11. Du, M., Yang, F., Zou, N., Hu, X.: Fairness in deep learning: a computational perspective. IEEE Intell. Syst. **36**(4), 25–34 (2021)

12. Dwork, C., Hardt, M., Pitassi, T., Reingold, O., Zemel, R.: Fairness through awareness. In: Proceedings of the 3rd Innovations in Theoretical Computer Science Conference, ITCS 2012, New York, NY, USA, pp. 214–226 (2012)
13. Fleisher, W.: What's Fair about Individual Fairness?. In: Proceedings of the 2021 AAAI/ACM Conference on AI, Ethics, and Society, New York, NY, USA, pp. 480–490 (2021)
14. Grote, T., Keeling, G.: On algorithmic fairness in medical practice. Camb. Q. Healthc. Ethics **31**(1), 83–94 (2022)
15. Hagler, D.J., et al.: Image processing and analysis methods for the Adolescent Brain Cognitive Development Study. Neuroimage **202**, 116091 (2019)
16. Herman-Giddens, M.E., et al.: Secondary sexual characteristics in boys: data from the Pediatric Research in Office Settings Network. Pediatrics **130**(5), e1058–1068 (2012)
17. Kearns, M., Neel, S., Roth, A., Wu, Z.S.: Preventing fairness gerrymandering: auditing and learning for subgroup fairness. In: International Conference on Machine Learning, pp. 2564–2572. PMLR (2018)
18. Larrazabal, A.J., Nieto, N., Peterson, V., Milone, D.H., Ferrante, E.: Gender imbalance in medical imaging datasets produces biased classifiers for computer-aided diagnosis. Proc. Natl. Acad. Sci. **117**(23), 12592–12594 (2020)
19. Martinez, N., Bertran, M., Sapiro, G.: Minimax pareto fairness: a multi objective perspective. In: Proceedings of the 37th International Conference on Machine Learning, pp. 6755–6764 (2020)
20. Pfohl, S., Marafino, B., Coulet, A., Rodriguez, F., Palaniappan, L., Shah, N.H.: Creating fair models of atherosclerotic cardiovascular disease risk. In: Proceedings of the 2019 AAAI/ACM Conference on AI, Ethics, and Society, pp. 271–278. Honolulu HI USA (2019)
21. Pohl, K.M., Thompson, W.K., Adeli, E., Linguraru, M.G. (eds.): Adolescent Brain Cognitive Development Neurocognitive Prediction. Lecture Notes in Computer Science, 1st edn. Springer, Cham (2019). https://doi.org/10.1007/978-3-030-31901-4
22. Puyol-Antón, E., et al.: Fairness in cardiac MR image analysis: an investigation of bias due to data imbalance in deep learning based segmentation. In: de Bruijne, M., et al. (eds.) MICCAI 2021. LNCS, vol. 12903, pp. 413–423. Springer, Cham (2021). https://doi.org/10.1007/978-3-030-87199-4_39
23. Selbst, A.D., Boyd, D., Friedler, S.A., Venkatasubramanian, S., Vertesi, J.: Fairness and abstraction in sociotechnical systems. In: 2019 Proceedings of the Conference on Fairness, Accountability, and Transparency, FAT* 2019, pp. 59–68. Association for Computing Machinery, New York (2019)
24. Seyyed-Kalantari, L., Zhang, H., McDermott, M.B.A., Chen, I.Y., Ghassemi, M.: Underdiagnosis bias of artificial intelligence algorithms applied to chest radiographs in under-served patient populations. Nat. Med. **27**(12), 2176–2182 (2021)
25. Stanley, E.A., Wilms, M., Mouches, P., Forkert, N.D.: Fairness-related performance and explainability effects in deep learning models for brain image analysis. J. Med. Imaging **9**, 061102 (2022)
26. Williams, D.R., Priest, N., Anderson, N.: Understanding associations between race, socioeconomic status and health: patterns and prospects. Health Psychol. Off. J. Div. Health Psychol. Am. Psychol. Assoc. **35**(4), 407–411 (2016)
27. Wu, T., Mendola, P., Buck, G.M.: Ethnic differences in the presence of secondary sex characteristics and menarche among US girls: the Third National Health and Nutrition Examination Survey, 1988–1994. Pediatrics **110**(4), 752–757 (2002)

28. Zhang, B.H., Lemoine, B., Mitchell, M.: Mitigating unwanted biases with adversarial learning. arXiv:1801.07593 (2018)
29. Zhang, H., Dullerud, N., Roth, K., Oakden-Rayner, L., Pfohl, S., Ghassemi, M.: Improving the fairness of chest X-ray classifiers. In: Proceedings of the Conference on Health, Inference, and Learning, pp. 204–233. PMLR (2022)

Separable vs. End-to-End Learning: A Critical Examination of Learning Paradigms

John S. H. Baxter[✉][iD]

Laboratoire Traitement du Signal et de l'Image (LTSI, INSERM UMR 1099),
Université de Rennes 1, Rennes, France
jbaxter@univ-rennes1.fr

Abstract. Machine learning is undoubtedly becoming more and more integrated into medical image computing research and practice. As with any conceptual or technological tool, this exposure requires the community to better understand the logical and philosophical foundations underpinning its use. One of the these (largely unexamined) areas is the *learning paradigm* that motivates everything from problem decomposition to architecture selection to clinical regulation. This article examines one of the spectra that defines the learning paradigm, specifically the spectrum between *end-to-end* and *separable learning*, in order to analyse what values drive solutions towards or away from either extreme.

Keywords: Machine learning · Values · Intermediate representations

1 Introduction

Deep learning has had an undeniable influence on research in medical image analysis with its focus on the construction of large-scale artificial neural networks to address innumerable areas of image processing. Early deep learning approaches, largely arising from natural image classification in computer vision, have dominated the public consciousness about how machine learning (ML) will eventually be used in medicine, with both researchers and speculative opinions from the wider public suggesting that machines will one day execute the complex diagnostic and interventional tasks currently performed by clinical teams.

Medical image computing is already crucial to solving these problems. It is easy to see that certain processing tasks, such as image reconstruction, hold a fundamental place in how medical images are understood, both by humans and by algorithms. What is more difficult to observe are the numerous other processes that images undergo in order to extract clinically usable information. For example, in a cancer monitoring context, images are reconstructed, the locations of tumours are determined, those tumours are segmented, those segmentations are measured in terms of size/volume/spiculatedness/etc. and the measurements are finally used for diagnostic decision support to infer if the cancer is malignant

J. S. H. Baxter et al. (Eds.): EPIMI 2022/ML-CDS 2022/TDA4BiomedicalImaging 2022,
LNCS 13755, pp. 26–37, 2022.
https://doi.org/10.1007/978-3-031-23223-7_3

or benign, growing or in remission. The conceptual separation of these tasks has been beneficial to the imaging research community, where individual groups can focus on more coherent and smaller pieces of the bigger picture.

One paradigm in deep learning has the explicit goal of challenging this. *End-to-end learning*, at its most extreme, encourages a single large (and often general) architecture to be used to address the entire pipeline from acquisition to medical outcome (e.g. diagnosis), without human-designed intermediate representations (IRs). This has been fuelled by recent advances both in ML and in the collection of *big data*, which is often unannotated except for the image and the medical outcome. An opposing idea is *separable learning* which posits that human-designed IRs are beneficial and ML should address the more discrete steps of transforming earlier representations into later ones, similar to medical image processing today.

The goal of this article is to critically examine the paradigms themselves through a theoretical lens, identifying them as a spectrum, and analysing the values that would drive a framework towards one or the other.

2 Nature as a Spectrum with Illustrative Examples

All ML frameworks are constructed within a *learning paradigm* that dictates their philosophical foundations. Certain aspects of the learning paradigm exist as spectra, such as the delineation between supervised and unsupervised learning or between loss-based vs. reinforcement learning, which are more commonly understood and discussed by ML researchers. Despite the seeming different worldviews of end-to-end and separable learning, they are actually two endpoints of a single spectrum (the end-to-end vs. separable spectrum or *E2ESS*) which can be understood through concrete examples.

As the positioning of an ML framework on the E2ESS can effects several technical aspects of the framework, very local examples where algorithm designers address the same problem in largely the same way illustrate the small technical differences that are indicative of their slightly difference positions on the E2ESS. For example, consider the approaches towards planning of deep brain stimulation of the subthalamic nucleus (STN) taken by Baxter *et al.* [5,6], Milletari *et al.* [22], and Zhao *et al.* [33]. These papers illustrate very similar approaches (i.e. convolutional neural networks (CNNs) applied to STN segmentation from preoperative MRI) whose differences largely arise from the differences in the paradigm they espouse more. (These methods as well as more extreme hypothetical approaches based on non-ML papers [23,29] are given in Fig. 1.) Each paper recognises the segmentation of small structures like the STN to be a difficult problem due to their small size despite their consistent anatomical location. The first two therefore conceptually separate the problem of determining the STN's rough location from the process of segmenting it (using the STN centroid co-ordinates as an IR), whereas Zhao *et al.* [33] takes a more traditionally end-to-end approach and doesn't make that distinction and uses a more general-purpose CNN. Milletari [22] and Baxter *et al.* [5,6] take different approaches to this separation. The former uses a single network to learn information about both the IR and the final segmentation simultaneously with a post-processing

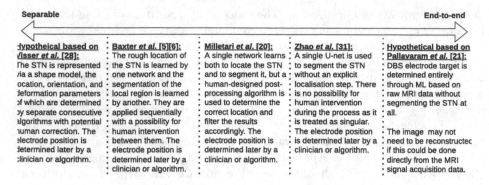

Fig. 1. End-to-end vs. separable spectrum for planning deep brain stimulation of the subthalamic nucleus using pre-operative MRI.

step to extract and integrate them. The latter uses different but more explicit networks consecutively for the IR and then the segmentation.

The more paradigmatically-extreme approaches differ from the three aforementioned ones in key ways. On the more separable-side, the problem of segmentation itself could be further separated by using parameterised models (i.e. with more IRs) of the STN (such as shape models [29]) which are themselves fit to the image in a separable way, (e.g. localisation followed by orientation followed by deformation). On the more extreme end-to-end side, the separation between STN segmentation and electrode positioning itself is questioned, and whether or not knowledge of the STN's exact boundary is useful for electrode positioning is left to the machine learning algorithm to determine. In an even more extreme example, one could imagine an algorithm doing this directly from the raw MRI acquisition rather than a separately reconstructed image, although to the best of our knowledge, no papers have yet to implement such an idea.

For another concrete example, consider the cardiac cine-MRI analysis frameworks proposed by Abdeltawab et al. [1], Khened et al. [19], Bai et al. [3], and Liu

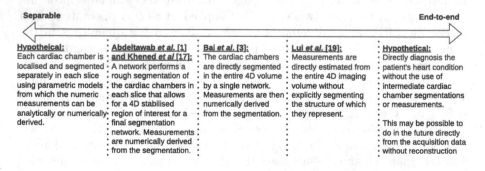

Fig. 2. End-to-end vs. separable spectrum for cardiac disorder diagnosis from MRI.

et al. [21] in which the segmented object's general location in the image as well as the segmentation itself are the principal IRs being varied. Each one focuses on determining numeric measurements of cardiac efficiency (such as left ventricular volume ejection fraction). Abdeltawab *et al.* [1] and Khened *et al.* [19] do so by estimating the location and extent of the left ventricle in the cine-MRI via a pre-segmentation network that allows them to crop the image to a region of interest for each time-step which is then given to a final left ventricular segmentation network, allowing them to calculate these quantitative measurements from the segmentation. Bai *et al.* [3] take a conceptually simple approach and use a single segmentation network applied on the whole image rather than a region of interest. (The measurements are again calculated from the segmentation.) Liu *et al.* remove the segmentation component altogether, directly estimating the ejection fraction as a regression problem. Figure 2 shows these methods and more paradigmatic hypothetical approaches along the E2ESS.

These examples illustrate that the difference between end-to-end and separable learning is that of degree and not type, with methods taking intermediate positions on the E2ESS. They also show that differences between positions on the E2ESS are exhibited through their architecture, processing, and problem representation, with a bias towards either end of the E2ESS having technical repercussions. Thus, we should examine the factors that influence how this bias is consciously or subconsciously determined by the ML framework designers.

3 Values Arising from Technical Considerations

3.1 Robustness and Reusability

One big concern in medical image processing is the robustness of algorithms towards patient and image variability. ML papers that use images from different scanners or are even agnostic to the parameters of image acquisition boast their capability to handle a wider variety of imaging contexts even if it does result in a small decrease in accuracy. But why?

There are two answers to this. The first is superficial: any patient population is heterogeneous and fundamentally contains noise and uncertainty. Being robust to this is unambiguously good. However, the second, deeper answer is that high robustness leads to reusability in different clinical contexts with lower cost to the healthcare system. This can already be seen with image acquisition systems: the same MRI bores are often used in clinic regardless if they are imagining heads or abdomens (what changes are the coils used which are significantly less expensive); the same ultrasound reconstruction and visualisation machines are used regardless of if they are imaging a fetus or a spine (what changes are the probes which again are smaller and less expensive).

This all appears to be clearly in favour of separable learning as each independent modules could be made independently more robust and reusable in different clinical contexts. The algorithms that take measurements from segmented anatomy do not have to concern themselves with the peculiarities of image reconstruction as the segmentation algorithm stands between the two. However, we have found no clear quantitative indication of this, and of the examples given in the previous section, the accuracy and performance differences between the methods are rather small when they are treated as fully-automatic.

End-to-end learning's approach to reuse instead involves the transfer of learned representations between similar problems, either through transfer learning or through multi-task learning. Provided that the architecture is not designed with too specific an application in mind, it can be appended with components either on the input side or the output side that could, even with a more limited data supply, reuse representations from other problems. This learning process must be augmented to avoid catastrophic forgetting [12], but there is no reason to believe that this cannot be overcome with future developments.

In this sense, it is the type of reuse that differs. Separable learning prioritises the more explicit, application-based reuse that one sees in more traditional software engineering which still dominates medical software. This is a type of *explicit reuse* in which the conditions of reuse are clear even if unstated (e.g. a brain MRI segmentation algorithm should be used only on segmenting brains in MR images, not some other anatomy in some other modality, but should be independent of what those segmentations will be used for). End-to-end learning on the other hand encourages *implicit reuse* which is more flexible (e.g. components of networks trained on classifying photographs of everyday things are now routinely used to pre-train parts of non-classification networks in medical imaging) but is also more uncertain and limited in terms of when it can be applied. Despite their names, there isn't a strict dichotomy between implicit and explicit reuse as having one doesn't necessarily prevent the other, e.g. one can still use transfer learning (implicit reuse) to train separable components for different problems (explicit reuse).

3.2   Dataset and Training Considerations

According to Jordan & Mitchell [17], one of the primary catalysts of the explosion of interest in neural networks for computer vision was the availability of large annotated databases such as ImageNet [10]. In medicine, such extremely large datasets are rare, but becoming increasingly available for certain problems in certain domains such as lesion detection [32], thoracic disease classification [30], and diagnosing knee disorders [7]. The commonality across these three large datasets is that they all exemplify classification problems in which the only annotations given are categorical tags (e.g. pathology, gender, etc.) or other simple continuous values (e.g. age, symptom measurements, etc.) rather than more intensive radiological annotations such as manual segmentations.

This means that data is more available for problems defined solely as classification or regression problems allowing these methods to make use of larger, more generic network architectures. This biases ML research towards end-to-end learning which is more likely to fit into this structure either by minimising additional labelling either on the input side or the output side. For example, if a disease is diagnosed through analysing a particular characteristic of a particular anatomical object, one would require a segmentation of said structure (either for input to an algorithm that does feature analysis or as a gold-standard reference for a segmentation algorithm) or take an end-to-end approach in which such a segmentation is not required [34]. This data also is easier to collect technically, as much of it is already stored in clinical PACS systems [2].

Thus data availability and ease-of-collection are clearly in favour of end-to-end learning, but the utility of a dataset is not only a question of raw size but also information content. As shown by the maintained interest in more singular, separable problems in the research community, there is still an advantage to annotating data with more complex, informative annotations for multiple steps in a complex processing pipeline. Additionally, data efficiency would affect utility, and appears that separable approaches tend to require smaller training datasets than the larger ones used in more clearly end-to-end frameworks. Annotation informativeness intuitively maintains a dichotomous relationship with ease-of-annotation; the former implies additional effort in annotation (i.e. adding more information to it) and the latter implies the inverse.

Once data has been collected for training and algorithm validation, there are still technical considerations that would lead a team to prefer one end of the spectrum over the other. *Federation* and the *distributedness* of the training process have recently become large concerns in medical image processing using ML as it tends to involve sensitive data from multiple clinical centres [26]. Given that federation tends to be applied to individually learned components, there isn't a theoretical difference between the two ends of the spectrum as the number of components (if trained quasi-independently) would have no relation to the degree to which any particular component could take advantage of a federated learning approach. However, there is a key difference in the capacity for distributed training, notably in favour of separable learning. This is because the separation between the learned components gives framework designers the ability to train them largely independently and thus distribute the training of the system seen as a whole. This is already trivially and unconsciously done to a extreme degree in the research community as different institutions/companies/laboratories specialise in different processes and train their algorithms completely independent of the others. There is no reason to believe that such a separation would be less feasible for a separated learning approach that maintains this distinction between sub-parts, but it is increasingly hard to imagine it with paradigmatic end-to-end approaches as they move further towards the physical image acquisition on one side and the medical outcome on the other.

3.3 Automation and Workflow Considerations

Although at a surface level, one would assume that automation would be solely in the purview of the end-to-end paradigm, but this is not the case in practice. The multiple separably-learned components are often executed automatically in a serial manner as illustrated by the more separable approaches in Sect. 2 being equally automatic as the end-to-end ones.

However, unlike automaticity, *interactivity* and *explainability* depend heavily on IRs to interact with that are human understandable [4]. Separable approaches can provide opportunities for human clinicians to observe the process and correct errors made by the different ML algorithms as well as making it necessarily more explainable. In his review of explainable ML, Preece [25] identifies the recent approaches with explainable ML with *post-hoc* interpretations that, even if they might help identify errors, still do not offer a mechanism for these errors to be easily corrected. Whether or not such explainable ML even helps identify errors is arguable due to potential cognitive overload when a human clinician must search through numerous machine-generated IRs that have not been learnt with interpretation in mind [13]. Despite this, they do have the promise of simplicity, a certain 'push-button' approach to complex medical image computing problems.

In terms of interactivity and explainability, image processing is heavily influenced by *logocentrism* as coined by early 20th century German philosopher, Ludwig Klages, which is the tendency in particular fields of knowledge to prioritise declarative (e.g. textual) language above other forms of representation, such as the visual or tonal, as a fundamental expression of an objective reality. Empirically, clinicians tend to prefer textual explanations over visual ones even when dealing with medical image ML [28]. For interactivity, the ability to explain the functioning an interaction mechanism (an inherently language-based task) is critical for its proper use [4]. Thus, both ends of the spectrum seem to be constrained by logocentrism, but end-to-end approaches are more-so, lacking the human-designed IRs that act as a convenient and logocentrically-available shortcuts into the inner workings of the ML approach.

3.4   Publishability Considerations

Publishability is obviously a pragmatic consideration for researchers due to the nature of their profession. In that respect, 'end-to-end' is also being increasing used as a keyword to attract readers in the title of papers. According to a PubMed search[1], the number of medical ML papers with 'end-to-end' in their title has increased exponentially since it was first used (only the once) in 2014 to now being used over 327 times, more than a third of those being from 2021. Obviously, the number of medical ML papers in that period is much larger but it is clear that the use of end-to-end learning is at least unconsciously seen as a net positive point towards publishability in a way that separable learning does not. (A similar search replacing 'end-to-end' with 'separable' yielded no results.) This may because of the novelty of the approach in the overall literature, with end-to-end methodologies being relatively new compared to the more conservative separable approach that predate deep learning.

A reason for this increased perception of publishability is the generally binary nature in which ML is presented to the public, with the wider public generally thinking of AI in terms of humans vs. machines (think of Hinton's famous

---

[1] Search string: "end-to-end" [Title] AND (neural[Title/Abstract] OR learned[Title/Abstract] or learning[Title/Abstract] OR deep[Title/Abstract]) NOT (neurorrhapy[Title/Abstract] OR anastomosis[Title/Abstract] OR nerve[Title/Abstract] OR esophagogastrostomy[Title/Abstract])", Search date: June 10, 2022.

comments about the end of radiology as a medical discipline) rather than collaborative [15,27]. As the end-to-end approach is canonically more independent of human users (unlike the more interaction-focused separable approach), it is reasonable to assume that people just entering the discipline through reading or contributing to the literature view it more from an end-to-end perspective. This is especially true in high-impact ML journals which must cater to a broad readership base with different interests even outside of medicine.

This does not strictly imply that end-to-end approaches are more publishable. In fact, the number of *domain-specialised* journals would suggest otherwise, as separable approaches could be piece-wise published in multiple forums. Also, because their problems are more specific, it is easier to find comparative methods and reference research results on which to compare rather than end-to-end approaches that do not have the capacity to investigate IRs in this manner. This is particularly true in medical imaging as the field contains a highly diverse collection of experts ranging from computer scientists to clinicians, many of which have disjoint intellectual priorities, background knowledge, and technical jargon. Thus, in practice, there appears to be a strong inverse relationship between the publishability that comes from domain-specialisation (i.e. focusing on the details of a restricted domain problem with the assumption of a large amount of domain knowledge on behalf of the reader) and from wider audience availability (i.e. focusing on 'the bigger picture' using language accessible to those outside of a particular domain, except perhaps machine learning or medical imaging itself).

3.5   Medical Knowledge Discovery

The primary motivation behind ML is to solve a particular pre-specified problem, as shown by the prevalence of supervised methods over unsupervised ones. In the context of end-to-end learning, the learned component is often seen as a 'black-box' even if efforts are taken towards improving explainability [25].

Logocentrism is again a factor in the relationship between ML and medical science. (Note the distinction between medical science, the process of determining knowledge about human health and well-being, and medicine, the process of improving human health and well-being through the diagnosis and treatment of illness.) Medical scientific knowledge, due to the textual nature of the literature, thus requires a linguistic representation of the results of image processing in aggregate. For an example of this, voxel-based analysis studies in neuroimaging almost uniformly textually describe their fundamentally image-based results in terms of the underlying anatomy, and meta-analyses of these studies tend to use this format exclusively [14,18,20,24]. This puts an additional hurdle in place for end-to-end learning: when the 'black-box' is opened, it seems likely to show deficits in the ML algorithm under analysis (such when COVID19 detection algorithms using radiographs are more sensitive to text superimposed on the images than to the images themselves [9]) which don't add to medical science whatsoever, although it may help future algorithm designers avoid specific shortcuts in later technical iterations. This complicates their use as an *a priori* causal understanding of the problem may still be necessary to determine when a finding is validly elucidating information about an underlying disorder (i.e. contributing to medical science) and when it is reflecting algorithmic shortcuts or other information off the causal path.

Separable algorithms again fare better in this respect because of the IRs themselves having a universally recognisable meaning outside of the algorithm that generates them. In an abstracted example, if one sees an article claiming that some measurement X of anatomy Y is positively correlated with disease state Z, the tendency tends to be on the format of the study or the results as a whole (i.e. the conceptual appropriateness or relatedness of X, Y, and Z; how patients and controls are selected and potential bias; the effect size and power of the study; whether or not it is multi-centre; etc.) rather than the accuracy of the algorithm used to segment Y in the image or the correctness of the algorithm that extracts the measurement of X. This is likely because those considerations are hidden by the framing (i.e. the *scope*) of the article itself, necessarily bracketing them in order to focus on its primary findings which are more accessible to the medical community that reads that particular journal.

This is a double-edged sword: although separable learning offers more readily accessible opportunities for medical knowledge discovery, it also fundamentally limits the potential scope of this knowledge compared to end-to-end algorithms which are conceptually free to creatively measure (or invent) new structures or features with a higher degree of flexibility and conceptual novelty. This use of deep neural networks is relatively new, but has yielded some interesting results that would otherwise go unnoticed due to their diversity or unexpectedness, such as sex differences in cardiac functionality unearthed via analysing an ML model applied to gender classification from EKG signals [16] or the CNN-derived non-local diffusion biomarkers of Parkinson's disease not detectable with traditional statistical analysis [11]. However, the discovered knowledge seems more difficult to communicate in a precise and reproducible manner, leading current methods to be more hypothesis-generating than hypothesis-answering. It is unclear if there can be a technological solution to this communication issue.

4 Conclusions

Table 1 summarises the many values logically affiliated with each end of the spectrum. These sometimes occur in opposing pairs (i.e. domain specialisation vs. general audience availability, or annotation informativeness vs. ease-of-collection) with an apparent trade-off. However, many exist in isolation, leading to a more complex system of trade-offs. To complicate matters, there are also numerous false differences, considerations that may superficially seem to apply specifically to either end of the spectrum but lack an empirical basis or deep theoretical rationale for such an affiliation.

As discussed by Ward [31] and several philosophers of science before her, it is difficult if not impossible to escape the non-epistemic values that unconsciously influence technical research. What we have shown here is that said values can themselves be technical (i.e. immediately related to the techniques used, such

Table 1. Values encoded in the end-to-end vs. separable learning spectrum

Separable learning	End-to-end learning
Reuse considerations	
Explicit reuse	Implicit reuse
Dataset and training considerations	
Annotation informativeness vs. Ease-of-annotation	
Data efficiency	Data availability
Distributedness	
Workflow considerations	
Explainability	Perceived simplicity
Interactivity	
Publication considerations	
Domain-specialisation vs. Wider audience availability	
Problem specificity	Perceived novelty
Knowledge discovery	
Accessibility	Novelty
Ease-of-extraction	Diversity
	Flexibility
False differences	
Accuracy	Data security & federation
Automation	

as ease-of-extraction, distributedness, reuse) or quasi-technical (i.e. indirectly related to the techniques used, such as knowledge diversity, explainability, simplicity). Of course, externally-non-technical (e.g. publishability) values appear as well, although at something of a greater distance due to the very broad and abstract nature of the spectrum under consideration. Although these types of values may often be invisible, unconscious, or implicit, they nevertheless play a crucial and central role in guiding ML framework development.

Thus, this analysis is missing a discussion of these more visible, externally-non-technical values that affect ML as a whole such as regulatory, economic, geopolitical, social, and environmental considerations. Superficially, they likely apply equally well to different ML frameworks regardless of their position on the end-to-end vs. separable spectrum and thus deserve separate analyses which demonstrate the technical and scientific factors influenced by them more immediately. For an example of one such analysis, Currie & Rohren [8] present an analysis of how racial factors affect the makeup of the problems addressed by ML in medical imaging and the corresponding datasets collected.

We hope that this exploration, however incomplete, will motivation ML researchers to more cognisant of the values that guide their most fundamental technological decisions. Through critically examining and questioning these values in practice, we hope they can be better aligned with those of clinical, industrial, and governmental collaborators as well as patients themselves, all of whom hold a stake in how patient care is achieved in the age of machine learning.

References

1. Abdeltawab, H., et al.: A deep learning-based approach for automatic segmentation and quantification of the left ventricle from cardiac cine MR images. Comput. Med. Imaging Graph. **81**, 101717 (2020)
2. Aiello, M., Cavaliere, C., D'Albore, A., Salvatore, M.: The challenges of diagnostic imaging in the era of big data. J. Clin. Med. **8**(3), 316 (2019)
3. Bai, W., et al.: Automated cardiovascular magnetic resonance image analysis with fully convolutional networks. J. Cardiovasc. Magn. Reson. **20**(1), 1–12 (2018)
4. Baxter, J.S.H., Gibson, E., Eagleson, R., Peters, T.M.: The semiotics of medical image segmentation. Med. Image Anal. **44**, 54–71 (2018)
5. Baxter, J.S.H., Maguet, E., Jannin, P.: Localisation of the subthalamic nucleus in MRI via convolutional neural networks for deep brain stimulation planning. In: Medical Imaging 2020: Image-Guided Procedures, Robotic Interventions, and Modeling, vol. 11315, p. 113150M. International Society for Optics and Photonics (2020)
6. Baxter, J.S.H., Maguet, E., Jannin, P.: Segmentation of the subthalamic nucleus in MRI via convolutional neural networks for deep brain stimulation planning. In: Medical Imaging 2021: Image-Guided Procedures, Robotic Interventions, and Modeling, vol. 11598, p. 115981K. International Society for Optics and Photonics (2021)
7. Bien, N., et al.: Deep-learning-assisted diagnosis for knee magnetic resonance imaging: development and retrospective validation of mrnet. PLoS Med. **15**(11), e1002699 (2018)
8. Currie, G., Rohren, E.: Social asymmetry, artificial intelligence and the medical imaging landscape. In: Seminars in Nuclear Medicine. Elsevier (2021)
9. DeGrave, A.J., Janizek, J.D., Lee, S.I.: AI for radiographic Covid-19 detection selects shortcuts over signal. Nat. Mach. Intell. **3**(7), 610–619 (2021)
10. Deng, J., Dong, W., Socher, R., Li, L.J., Li, K., Fei-Fei, L.: ImageNet: a large-scale hierarchical image database. In: 2009 IEEE Conference on Computer Vision and Pattern Recognition, pp. 248–255. IEEE (2009)
11. Estudillo-Romero, A., Haegelen, C., Jannin, P., Baxter, J.S.: Voxel-based Diktiometry-combining convolutional neural networks with voxel-based analysis and its application in diffusion tensor imaging for Parkinson's disease. medRxiv (2022)
12. French, R.M.: Catastrophic forgetting in connectionist networks. Trends Cogn. Sci. **3**(4), 128–135 (1999)
13. Ghassemi, M., Oakden-Rayner, L., Beam, A.L.: The false hope of current approaches to explainable artificial intelligence in health care. Lancet Digit. Health **3**(11), e745–e750 (2021)
14. Gong, J., et al.: Common and distinct patterns of intrinsic brain activity alterations in major depression and bipolar disorder: voxel-based meta-analysis. Transl. Psychiatry **10**(1), 1–13 (2020)
15. Gupta, S., Kattapuram, T.M., Patel, T.Y.: Social media's role in the perception of radiologists and artificial intelligence. Clin. Imaging **68**, 158–160 (2020)
16. Hicks, S.A., et al.: Explaining deep neural networks for knowledge discovery in electrocardiogram analysis. Sci. Rep. **11**(1), 1–11 (2021)
17. Jordan, M.I., Mitchell, T.M.: Machine learning: trends, perspectives, and prospects. Science **349**(6245), 255–260 (2015)

18. Keramatian, K., Chakrabarty, T., Saraf, G., Pinto, J.V., Yatham, L.N.: Grey matter abnormalities in first-episode mania: a systematic review and meta-analysis of voxel-based morphometry studies. Bipolar Disord. **23**(3), 228–240 (2021)
19. Khened, M., Kollerathu, V.A., Krishnamurthi, G.: Fully convolutional multi-scale residual densenets for cardiac segmentation and automated cardiac diagnosis using ensemble of classifiers. Med. Image Anal. **51**, 21–45 (2019)
20. Liu, X., et al.: Gray matter structures associated with neuroticism: a meta-analysis of whole-brain voxel-based morphometry studies. Hum. Brain Mapping (2021)
21. Liu, Z., Zhang, Y., Li, W., Li, S., Zou, Z., Chen, B.: Multislice left ventricular ejection fraction prediction from cardiac MRIs without segmentation using shared SptDenNet. Comput. Med. Imaging Graph. **86**, 101795 (2020)
22. Milletari, F., et al.: Hough-CNN: deep learning for segmentation of deep brain regions in MRI and ultrasound. Comput. Vis. Image Underst. **164**, 92–102 (2017)
23. Pallavaram, S., D'Haese, P.F., Lake, W., Konrad, P.E., Dawant, B.M., Neimat, J.S.: Fully automated targeting using nonrigid image registration matches accuracy and exceeds precision of best manual approaches to subthalamic deep brain stimulation targeting in Parkinson disease. Neurosurgery **76**(6), 756–765 (2015)
24. Pan, N., et al.: Brain gray matter structures associated with trait impulsivity: a systematic review and voxel-based meta-analysis. Hum. Brain Mapp. **42**(7), 2214–2235 (2021)
25. Preece, A.: Asking 'why' in AI: explainability of intelligent systems-perspectives and challenges. Intell. Syst. Acc. Financ. Manag. **25**(2), 63–72 (2018)
26. Rieke, N., et al.: The future of digital health with federated learning. NPJ Digit. Med. **3**(1), 1–7 (2020)
27. Stai, B., et al.: Public perceptions of artificial intelligence and robotics in medicine. J. Endourol. **34**(10), 1041–1048 (2020)
28. Tonekaboni, S., Joshi, S., McCradden, M.D., Goldenberg, A.: What clinicians want: contextualizing explainable machine learning for clinical end use. In: Machine Learning for Healthcare Conference, pp. 359–380. PMLR (2019)
29. Visser, E., Keuken, M.C., Forstmann, B.U., Jenkinson, M.: Automated segmentation of the substantia Nigra, subthalamic nucleus and red nucleus in 7 t data at young and old age. Neuroimage **139**, 324–336 (2016)
30. Wang, X., Peng, Y., Lu, L., Lu, Z., Bagheri, M., Summers, R.M.: ChestX-ray8: hospital-scale chest X-ray database and benchmarks on weakly-supervised classification and localization of common thorax diseases. In: Proceedings of the IEEE Conference on Computer Vision and Pattern Recognition, pp. 2097–2106 (2017)
31. Ward, Z.B.: On value-laden science. Stud. Hist. Philos. Sci. Part A **85**, 54–62 (2021)
32. Yan, K., Wang, X., Lu, L., Summers, R.M.: DeepLesion: automated mining of large-scale lesion annotations and universal lesion detection with deep learning. J. Med. Imaging **5**(3), 036501 (2018)
33. Zhao, W., et al.: Automated segmentation of midbrain structures in high-resolution susceptibility maps based on convolutional neural network and transfer learning. Front. Neurosci. **16** (2022)
34. Zhen, X., Li, S.: Towards direct medical image analysis without segmentation. arXiv preprint arXiv:1510.06375 (2015)

A 35-Year Longitudinal Analysis of Dermatology Patient Behavior Across Economic and Cultural Manifestations in Tunisia, and the Impact of Digital Tools

Mohamed Akrout[3](✉), Hayet Amdouni[1], Amal Feriani[1], Monia Kourda[2], and Latif Abid[3]

[1] M.B. Dermatology Clinic, Bizerte, Tunisia
[2] Department of Dermatology, Razi Hospital, Manouba, Tunisia
[3] AIPLabs/AIPDerm, Budapest, Hungary
mohamed@aip.ai

Abstract. The evolution of behavior of dermatology patients has seen significantly accelerated change over the past decade, driven by surging availability and adoption of digital tools and platforms. Through our longitudinal analysis of this behavior within Tunisia over a 35-year time frame, we identify behavioral patterns across economic and cultural dimensions and how digital tools have impacted those patterns in preceding years. Throughout this work, we highlight the witnessed effects of available digital tools as experienced by patients, and conclude by presenting a vision for how future tools can help address the issues identified across economic and cultural manifestations. Our analysis is further framed around three types of digital tools: "Dr. Google", social media, and artificial intelligence (AI) tools, and across three stages of clinical care: pre-visit, in-visit, and post-visit.

Keywords: Dermatology · e-Health technology · Reverse image search · Social media groups · AI tools

1 Introduction

In this accelerating and expanding digital age, information technologies and image processing techniques have thrown us into an inevitable "iconosphere" whose psychological, epistemological, and cultural impacts are undeniable [13]. Amongst the various industries where the digital age has transformed the respective processes, products, and services, healthcare has significantly lagged all other industries despite it having the greatest potential, both in terms of the ability to fundamentally improve the delivery of care as well as the overall impact of that to civilization. Despite the connectivity potential and advanced digitization in this new age, patients are still at the mercy of inaccessibility to accurate clinical care in a timely or convenient manner. The potential transformative impact of

J. S. H. Baxter et al. (Eds.): EPIMI 2022/ML-CDS 2022/TDA4BiomedicalImaging 2022,
LNCS 13755, pp. 38–50, 2022.
https://doi.org/10.1007/978-3-031-23223-7_4

this digital age is especially exciting, yet thus far disappointing, in lower socio-economic regions of the world, where economic and cultural barriers uniquely inhibit patients' access to the requisite care.

A patient's healthcare "journey" has been significantly impacted by software technology [7]. Patient "empowerment" has been augmented due to the easy capture of skin lesions, taken by mobile phones or digital cameras from a distance, and the proliferation of those "macroscopic" images in search engines and social media. This empowerment by technological advances is disseminated and encouraged by the media, which is driving patients to be more demanding in their education and in the vocalization of their care with their physicians.

With healthcare challenges facing the world significantly worsened by COVID, there is an increasing imperative to better analyze and understand how digital tools can transform healthcare across various economic and culturally distinct regions. To effectively design and deploy such tools, it is important that we analyze historical patient behavior across the three clinical stages (pre-, in-, and post-visit) over an extended time frame, and in unique cultural and economic landscapes. This is especially the case in underdeveloped countries such as Tunisia, where healthcare services have more primitive infrastructure and resources. In these regions, digital adoption further lags more developed regions but there is greater potential to improve the current standard of care and address unique economic and cultural barriers [4,16].

By studying patient behavior over the last 35 years through the consistent lens of two leading dermatologists in Tunisia, we identified that the first 25 of the 35 years mainly experienced slow and minimal change. However, the last 10 years witnessed a significant change due to the introduction of expansive digital tools such as social media, Google search, reverse image searches, and AI tools. Over that time frame, we also witnessed an economic shift in Tunisia after the revolution in 2010–2011, and a significant deterioration in the average household income and level of access and quality of both public and private healthcare. This paper makes the following contributions:

- We describe the change in patients' behavior over 35 years in Tunisia, segmented into two periods of 1987–2012 and 2012–2022, and we pattern this behavior across coinciding economic and cultural environments.
- We discuss and highlight the witnessed effects of digital tools on patient behavior and incorporate that impact across the three stages of clinical care (pre-, in-, and post-visit).
- We present a case for how we envision digital tools, such as "AIPDerm", can positively address Tunisia's, and similar regions', economic and cultural issues, as well as significantly evolve the current standard of how digital tools impact the patient's behavior across the three clinical stages.

2   35 Years of Dermatology Patient Behavior Across All Three Clinic Stages

We analyze patient behavior in a single region of Tunisia across 35 years by examining the direct experiences of two dermatologists who continuously practiced in the region over that period. We segment the observed patient behaviors and perceptions into the three clinical stages: pre-, in-, and post-visit. Within each segment, we analyze the shift of those behaviors and perceptions over the 35-year period, and more specifically, the more notable period of 2012–2022.

2.1   Pre-visit Perception

Preceding the knowledge-at-your-fingertips era of search engines, it was significantly difficult to access any breadth or depth of medical information, constraining patients to almost exclusively trust the diagnosis of the dermatologist. Following the launch and evolution of search engines, patients were more quickly catalyzed at the slightest illness manifestation or concern, with patients now empowered to match their symptoms and be pre-emptively guided on the possible diagnoses, the urgency of the pathology, and the therapeutic possibilities. This empowerment of manually navigating search engines for textual matching of symptoms and conditions has more recently evolved into taking photos of their skin lesions and using reverse image search functionality to find cases with similar visual representations and the corresponding possible skin diagnoses.

Around the 2010–2011 period, Facebook gained significant scale and reach in Tunisia, with this adoption having been validated extensively in the press and public domain given the pivotal role it played in the Tunisian and other "Arab Spring" uprisings [3]. On the dermatology side, Tunisian citizens are constantly engaged on Facebook groups to exchange opinions at different engagement levels about *i*) existing medical prescriptions from prior medical visits, *ii*) personal judgment about the personality, professionalism, availability, and expertise of the respective dermatologist, and *iii*) personal experiences with specific treatments for a given pathology (e.g., acne).

While these discussions can represent useful natural language processing datasets for future AI tools and guide the design of clinical trial recruitment, prevention campaigns, and chronic disease management [5], the quality of shared medical information on social media suffers from the lack of reliability and confidentiality [10]. As the working class's household income and purchasing power have been falling since the 2010–2011 revolution, many patients rely on their discussions on social media to self-educate and self-medicate, exposing patients to various risks such as mistreatment and triggering rashes or drug toxicity. This is in contrast to the pre-digital stronghold era (maturity of search engines and scale-up of social platforms), which had materially lower risk exposure of erroneous and dangerous self-education or self-medication, and where dermatologists were granted more exclusive trust in medical determinations. In order to mitigate some of these risks and limitations with basic self-education, Tunisian website alternatives (e.g., med.tn, tobba.tn) offer a dedicated medical forum where subscribed doctors can answer medical questions posted by patients. However, doctors are asked to not provide a specific diagnosis, with their answers instead of revolving around reporting the severity of the patient's case, thus providing a more triaging type of guidance.

Certain skin conditions can be embarrassing or culturally sensitive, such as sexually transmitted diseases (e.g., venereal vegetations, genital herpes, genital candidiasis), which have been, and continue to be, very taboo culturally in Tunisian society. In these cases, most Tunisian patients have notably preferred sending a photo of their lesion accompanied by a textual description of symptoms. This optionality is something that has been enabled by the availability of mobile devices and platforms, and whose absence rendered a significant proportion of the population at the mercy of rigid cultural norms, often resulting in undiagnosed or untreated conditions.

2.2 In-Visit Perception

Across the clinical time frame of 35 years of experience, we had extensive exposure to both public hospitals and private clinics in Tunisia. We characterize the profile and mindset of dermatology patients during medical visits and classify them into the following (with potential overlapping) categories.

Patients with Higher Education Background. This category includes patients with higher-education and scientific backgrounds (e.g., engineers, physicians, architects) or with a background in studying advanced literature (e.g., lawyers, journalists, judges, administrative executives). They expect the dermatologist to direct them towards the right etiological and therapeutic approach after they self-administered and pre-established a survey about their symptoms and possible diagnosis from Google searches and other digital tools. They also keep track of high-resolution images and videos of their skin lesions (e.g., angioedema and urticaria) which simplify and accelerate the diagnostic process of the dermatologist. This category of patients perceives the role of dermatologists as the only single and final source of providing trustworthy diagnoses and treatments. These patient profiles also tend not to over-argue or question the dermatologist's determination of appropriate next steps and treatments (e.g., blood test before drug prescription).

Patients with Limited Income. This category is the one that significantly utilizes social media and Google searches, with those tools most impacting their patient journey through the three clinical stages. These patients try to actively avoid paying medical consultation fees and can excessively opt for self-medication until a friend or pharmacist urges them to consult a dermatologist (e.g., in front of a mole growing in size out of concern of a melanoma diagnosis) or until their condition worsens. For most witnessed patients in this category, dermatologists in Tunisia are seen as the last resort after exhausting all self-medication methods. Over the past decade and with the worsening economic landscape since the 2010–2011 revolution, there has been an increase in patients that fit into this category and who actively seek to avoid the medical fees of multiple visits. We have noticed that they tend to consult a dermatologist for aggregated medical concerns within a single medical visit, which implies that they are allowing for a build-up of illness and manifestations over an extended period of time before acquiescing to paying for fees associated with a single visit. They view this as allowing them to obtain a "multiple treatment package" without the intention of treating each of the skin diseases properly and within the appropriate time frame. However, this practice is not prohibited by Tunisian law and tends to drive awkwardness during dermatologist interactions.

Patients Who Already "Know" the Diagnosis. While it is true that a diagnosis can sometimes seem obvious (e.g., vitiligo, common wart, acne, or burn), patients can often have overly inflated confidence in some of these cases and unnecessarily argue with dermatologists on their medical decisions. The patient consults to ensure possible therapeutic arrangements, their effectiveness, and their aesthetic aspects. Patients often perceive the role of dermatologists as one that is oriented toward frequent follow-ups and very personalized medical advice, without which the patient is not satisfied. This is because the patient can unintentionally not consider the dermatologist's actual core diagnosis as part of the overall medical visit. The role of the dermatologist is to reassure the patient and track them regularly according to the severity of the disease, its location, its extent, and its treatment punctuality. Given that patients can be overconfident about their diagnosis, they tend to ask questions to better understand any discrepancy between the dermatologist's opinion and what they have read on social media or "Dr. Google". Questions such as "we know the diagnosis, so why are you asking for a blood test?" or "I saw similar photos to my case on Facebook; why are you complicating my case?" are not uncommon.

Patients with Skin Conditions in Intimate Body Locations. Patients in Tunisia having genital skin lesions often refuse to be physically examined in person. They usually come with multiple photos taken before their visit and expect the dermatologist to give a prescription purely based on analyzing the pre-captured photos, as they believe that "they have nothing else", and that it must be sufficient for the medical examination. This request goes against the medical code of ethics but is common behavior in Tunisia given the cultural backdrop and sensitivity in the region around intimate body locations and taboo topics such as sexual activity and disease contraction. These embarrassing situations can leave doctors with a dilemma, and often find themselves engaged in a time-consuming cultural discussion in order to convince the patient into accepting the appropriate medical examination. For example, in the case of Behcet's disease, when a patient photographs their genital ulcers and asks the dermatologist for the therapeutic solution without being examined, the dermatologist must explain to the patient that it is imperative to inspect for medical ulcers, pseudo-folliculitis, and even carry out a neurological examination. Predictably, based on the cultural and sexual sensitivities on this front, our discussions with both male and female dermatologists in Tunisia confirm that this scenario is especially frequent when the patient and dermatologist are of opposite genders. In general, we observe that patients in Tunisia actively seek to validate their skin conditions in intimate locations by sending their photos via messaging apps before being obliged to visit the dermatologist in-person. It is worth noting that dermatologists may find themselves in various delicate situations that could give rise to legal interventions, such as the case of a molluscum of the perianal region of a child suggesting sexual abuse. In such medico-legal situations, taking photos becomes imperative and mandatory, but can also be problematic in front of some parents who opposite it in order to avoid cultural shame and stigmas.

Uncooperative Patients. Patients with lower intellectual levels, educational backgrounds, or with limited job and career prospects, are often seen spending time on Facebook groups and other social media platforms looking for depigmenting miracle creams for their melasma, and doing so without the more basic concern of worrying about having a sunscreen protecting against ultraviolet type A (UVA), ultraviolet type B (UVB) and blue light. Some of these patients are often seen consulting dermatologists to "achieve" their cosmetic dreams that they conjured in their imaginations through sporadic reading of various online sources, and thus have established unreasonably high expectations on what can be achieved and over short periods of treatment [15]. In such cases, many patients are quick to claim that the treatment must not be effective. It has therefore proven prudent for dermatologists in Tunisia to take regular photos showing the temporal evolution of the disease, and present those depictions as clear visually convincing evidence whenever the patient questions the improvement of their skin condition or the inefficacy of the prescribed treatment. Figure 1 depicts the case of a patient who visited his hairdresser to shave his beard. The hairdresser suggested to the patient to stop the nevus's volume from increasing by surrounding it with a line of a fishing rod. Figure 1a shows the photo of the patient during his first medical visit where the nevus is surrounded by a line of a fishing rod. The nevus shown in Fig. 1b illustrates its evolution after two months of treatment. The patient claimed that the state of his nevus did not improve, yet it was sufficient for the dermatologist to show him his photo in Fig. 1a from his first visit to convince him of the improvement.

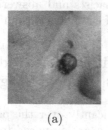 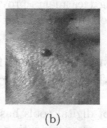

(a)   (b)

Fig. 1. An image of a nevus surrounded by a line of a fishing rod in (a) and its evolution after two months of treatment in (b).

2.3 Post-visit Perception

Patient follow-ups can be almost as important as the actual medical visit, given that they help ensure patients have adhered to their treatments and in tracking the treatments' effects. Given the observed historical tendency for patients to potentially neglect in-person follow-ups, digital tools have shown utility in enabling convenient remote check-ins for post-visit care and tracking. For example, the patient can use digital tools to send images of the progress of their burn to their dermatologist, allowing for remote monitoring as well as treatment adjustments if necessary. A distinct phenomenon observed in Tunisia is related to the differences between the prescribed treatment by dermatologists (and doctors in general) and the one ultimately provided by pharmacists. These differences can be due to the lack of availability of specific drugs or brands in pharmacies, which is a simple and logical justification. However, the most common reason for the difference in what is prescribed is explained by the unfortunate unfolding competition between pharmacists, who can withhold patients' prescriptions until the unavailable drugs are in-stock again, even though the specifically needed drugs are already available in other pharmacies. In such situations, the ideal patient contacts the dermatologist to verify if the drugs they obtained from the pharmacist are equivalent to the ones prescribed. However, due to the lack of sensitivity and awareness in most cases, the patients will start their treatment without giving adequate attention to the changes in the prescription made by their pharmacists. Given these more nuanced and technical problems, which are seldom present in more developed countries, dermatologists in Tunisia often find themselves playing the role of "medical policeman". For example, the dermatologist can instruct their patient to take a photo of their treatment before beginning to use it to allow for the dermatologist to confirm what has been issued by the pharmacist. A similar issue with cosmetic products that has become more prevalent in recent years is when a patient exchanges drugs with friends, especially when dealing with budget limitations, thereby neglecting the specific prescribed dosage of drugs from the dermatologist for a personalized and optimal therapeutic result. From this perspective, the perceived role of dermatologists revolves around checking treatments provided by pharmacists and answering any questions, which is often expected for free in cases of complications and uncertainty.

3 The Historical Evolution of Digital Tools and Their Patient-Behavior Impact Across Clinical Stages

The adoption of digital tools has evolved significantly over the past ten years, with distinct progress impacting patient behavior as compared to the 25 years prior to that. However, the full potential of digital tools in the healthcare industry is still far from being realized, with historical implementations largely centering around broader communication and information accessing platforms. While this improves patients' access to any kind of relevant medical information and provides the opportunity to discuss with fellow patients, these tools can be very high in risk of mis-education or mis-treatment, and can hinder dermatologists' efforts in providing optimal care. We investigate "Dr. Google", social media, and AI tools, the three major digital tools that were used over the last 10 years in Tunisia, and assess their impact across the clinical stages.

3.1 Social Media

The usage of social media in Tunisia, in particular Facebook, has undergone an astonishing growth over the last ten years, and today, Facebook drives 92.65% of Tunisian social media traffic in the month of June 2022, with similar levels over the last 12 months; Facebook's dominance significantly beats other platforms in that category which includes YouTube, Twitter, Instagram, Pinterest, LinkedIn, Reddit, and other platforms [1]. Popular applications such as Facebook, Messenger, and Instagram are freely and instantly accessible and provide user-friendly platforms to search and share medical information. Further, Tunisian patients also rely on Facebook groups and pages to seek other patients' opinions and ratings of different dermatologists or clinics. Such platforms offer support systems where disease-focused groups or communities can be created to share experiences and provide psychological support. Facebook and Messenger usage is not restricted to patients, dermatologists also utilize such tools to discuss and solicit each other's opinions and potential diagnoses on more complex or ambiguous cases [9]. Furthermore, social media, and messaging apps facilitate useful patient-doctor and doctor-doctor communications. If the doctor has an online presence, such tools can be used to provide clinic communications, virtual assistance and facilitate follow-ups. Social media platforms have been generally used by Tunisian dermatologists to raise awareness, encourage preventive or misguided behaviors, and offer advice and information on skin diseases to help minimize the risks of self-education and self-treatment. However, the availability of dermatologists to directly regulate content on such platforms is minimal, and their impact is unscalable given the broad usage of those platforms by the general population.

Unfortunately, social media is not always a reliable source of information, especially with complex and highly-personalized diagnoses and treatments, and has been shown to quite easily and quickly disseminate false or misleading information to widespread audiences. Such platforms are often used by commercial organizations or sales-representatives seeking to aggressively promote products for profit, which can lead to harmful misinformation or consequences [14].

3.2 "Dr. Google"

Search engine market share in Tunisia is heavily dominated by Google, with 94.95% of the total search engine market as of June 2022 [1]. With around 72% of residents having access to the internet, and with over 90% of the population having at least one mobile phone, accessibility to the internet and information is quite high, enabling most patients to consult the internet before visiting a dermatologist. Patients usually seek information through searching their symptoms or using more advanced search tools like reverse image searches. The latter is a software tool that enables users to find visually similar images simply by uploading a photograph of the skin lesion. While these tools are used in both developed and underdeveloped countries, dermatologists in Tunisia have emphasized that patients in underdeveloped or economically challenged regions, such as Tunisia, have been driven to rely heavily on these online tools to solely self-medicate, deferring a consult with a specialist to when symptoms significantly deteriorate or misalign with their self-diagnosis.

The ability for patients to seek medical information through various online search engines outside their clinical visit can be beneficial but can also pose significant risks. Self-educating through online resources can facilitate more comprehensive communication between patients and dermatologists, encourage the patient to ask more questions, alert the dermatologist to relevant aspects of their case, and become more engaged with their treatment across the clinical stages. However, the vast amount of information online can be overwhelming, and the ability to ascertain an accurate online diagnosis is low and dangerous, yet is unfortunately still relied upon by patients in deferring visits, especially in less developed or economically challenged countries.

3.3   The First AI Tools

AI is playing a pivotal role in advancing e-health solutions for dermatology [2,8,11]. Dermatology is a suitable high-value use case for AI, as it is a visual-dependent specialty and given that numerous image recognition algorithms have already been proven to be effective in detecting skin diseases and cancers [6]. This progress in AI has also fueled the design of several web or mobile image-based diagnosis apps for skin conditions such as "AIPDerm", which has had significant success in Europe. These AI-based tools are beneficial for various expertise levels within a clinic, from senior dermatologists to junior nurses, and help distinguish possible skin conditions and provide more sophisticated differential diagnosis possibilities along with ancillary information. AI-based diagnostic tools also play an important role in teledermatology given that they can help patients avoid long waiting periods and pre-identify and triage the severity of their skin condition.

Currently, most dermatologists in Tunisia do not use AI tools for a second opinion. We asked more than 300 dermatologists about their reasons for not yet adopting AI tools, and more than 96% were worried about the following two aspects of these applications:

- *Privacy concerns about users' health data*: most applications indicate they would not use uploaded images to target advertising, and would only save them to further train their classification algorithms, if users gave them explicit permission to do so. However, dermatologists in Tunisia do not have a legal framework established for digital dermatology, and at this early juncture, still feel insecure about adopting these applications.
- *Limited coverage of skin diseases*: most dermatology AI applications are limited in scope of capabilities as they are narrowly targeted toward specific skin

diseases such as skin cancers. In other words, they do not cover a wide enough diagnostic capability supporting the majority of skin diseases and cancers.

Remote triaging solutions based on AI tools offer the potential for addressing challenges in many low- and middle-income countries in Africa, or similar economic and culturally inhibiting regions, especially if offered at scale [12]. However, the need for in-person visits remains irreplaceable in many cases, and where the need for precise and nuanced knowledge of medical context is critical. Figure 2 shows one of those cases where the back of the patient has well-defined, painless but itchy, multiple lesions, such as scratches, ulcerations, or cuts. The patient uses a brush to scratch her back. All AI applications we have tested failed this case as it looks like skin picking. This is because the correct diagnosis, pathomimia (a.k.a., factitious dermatosis), is self-induced and often difficult to find if the dermatologist does not consider the psychological profile of the patient, which is confirmed by the opinion of the psychiatrist.

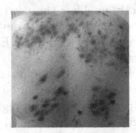

Fig. 2. The back of a patient with pathomimia disease triggered by a psychological concern.

4 The Future: How Can Advanced Digital Tools Optimize Patient Behavior Across All Clinical Stages and Address Economic and Cultural Barriers?

Although we have witnessed transformative evolutions in digital connectivity tools over the last few decades, healthcare remains stagnated in a world of under-adoption and misutilization. The available tools are constantly evolving to be far more sophisticated and tailored than the basic platforms broadly used today. We have begun to see the potential of these future tools in addressing the weakness and limitations of past tools, as global efforts in developing dermatology AI tools have been substantial. With respect to the future capabilities of AI systems, we believe its core features should address the patient care and digital tool issues described in this paper. One of the issues is dangerous self-education, and the vast degree of error and risk associated with that. With a system that utilizes sophisticated diagnosis AI modules such as a visual image diagnosis system, the system can minimize the associated error risk by providing a highly accurate diagnostic tool that is not at the mercy of patient diligence. It can be accessed by patients, with results sent to the clinic for oversight, and used as a high-confidence triaging and education tool benefiting both the pre-visit and in-visit stages. For the post-visit stage, a patient management platform can offer a patient portal that provides direct information about their diagnosis and treatments along with detailed reference material for contextual explanations, minimizing the possibility of speculation, skepticism, and non-adherence. This platform can also provide the ability for patients to asynchronously submit questions to the clinic regarding any concerns, minimizing misinformation and ensuring patient actions and understandings are carefully managed by the clinic. This system will also minimize patients' delays in addressing a possible ailment due to economic reasons and false confidence from self-education, by instantly providing a sophisticated triage and education tool at no incremental overhead costs due to its scalability. The system will also allow dermatologists and their staff to focus their efforts on management and oversight of a single platform while allowing for the ability to follow up with patients on obtaining correct prescriptions and subsequent treatment adherence, as well as enable remote condition monitoring post-visit, which more efficiently qualifies the need for future in-person visits. Such a system has already been comprehensively developed, clinically validated, and successfully deployed at a country-wide level in Europe – "AIPDerm", which is based in Hungary and Spain.

Economically, in regions where fiscal stability is sensitive, we believe the scalability and accessibility of such platforms can be transformative. Culturally, we believe such a system is especially relevant in regions such as Tunisia, where longstanding cultural norms and sensitivities can inhibit the requisite treatment for many. In such regions, this can manifest within households where female members can be prohibited from seeing a physician by the male patriarch of the family on the basis of privacy, protection, and cultural sensitivities. We believe that the system can help mitigate such issues by allowing patients to localize the lesion in an image, minimize the inclusion of other body parts, and not require the patient's physical presence, allowing for remote triaging of their case. Overall, we believe this envisioned system can largely solve the aforementioned patient behavior issues, including cultural and economic constraints, and reduce the perversion of existing basic tools and social media platforms.

5   Conclusion

Patient behavior in dermatology has undergone significant changes over the past 35 years, predominantly over the last decade, driven by significant transformation and adoption of digital tools. Patient behavior is analyzed across three clinical stages: pre-visit, in-visit, and post-visit, and is classified into several profiles that reflect observed patient behaviors. The causes of different patients' behaviors are not singular and this work illuminates the predominantly witnessed patterns in Tunisia. Digital tools have materially impacted how patients behave in all three clinical stages, with various economic and cultural aspects specific to Tunisia also contributing to the patterned patient behavior. While basic digital tools have exposed patients to risks of self-education and self-medication, there is clear potential in minimizing those risks and in mitigating the economic and cultural concerns of Tunisia and various regions globally. The aim of this paper was to describe patient behavior over 35 years in Tunisia across the three clinical stages, while analyzing the coinciding effects of economic and cultural manifestations, and the overarching impact of digital tools. We culminated by detailing how digital tools can mitigate Tunisia's, and similar regions', economic and cultural constraints, and how specific innovations can significantly evolve the current standard of how digital tools impact patient behaviors and outcomes.

References

1. Statcounter Global Stats. https://gs.statcounter.com/search-engine-market-share/. Accessed 20 June 2022
2. Akrout, M., Farahmand, A., Jarmain, T., Abid, L.: Improving skin condition classification with a visual symptom checker trained using reinforcement learning. In: Shen, D., et al. (eds.) MICCAI 2019. LNCS, vol. 11767, pp. 549–557. Springer, Cham (2019). https://doi.org/10.1007/978-3-030-32251-9_60
3. Allagui, I., Kuebler, J.: The Arab spring and the role of ICTs| introduction. Int. J. Commun. **5**, 8 (2011)
4. Azevedo, M.J.: The state of health system(s) in Africa: challenges and opportunities. In: Azevedo, M.J. (ed.) Historical Perspectives on the State of Health and Health Systems in Africa, Volume II. AHM, pp. 1–73. Springer, Cham (2017). https://doi.org/10.1007/978-3-319-32564-4_1
5. Della Rosa, S., Sen, F., et al.: Health topics on Facebook groups: content analysis of posts in multiple sclerosis communities. Interact. J. Med. Res. **8**(1), e10146 (2019)
6. Esteva, A., et al.: Dermatologist-level classification of skin cancer with deep neural networks. Nature **542**(7639), 115–118 (2017)
7. Ginige, J.A., Maeder, A.J.: Transforming Healthcare Through Innovation in Digital Health: Selected Papers from Global Telehealth 2018, vol. 254. IOS Press (2018)
8. Gomolin, A., Netchiporouk, E., Gniadecki, R., Litvinov, I.V.: Artificial intelligence applications in dermatology: where do we stand? Front. Med. **7**, 100 (2020)
9. Masoni, M., Guelfi, M.R.: Whatsapp and other messaging apps in medicine: opportunities and risks. Intern. Emerg. Med. **15**(2), 171–173 (2020)
10. Moorhead, S.A., Hazlett, D.E., Harrison, L., Carroll, J.K., Irwin, A., Hoving, C.: A new dimension of health care: systematic review of the uses, benefits, and limitations of social media for health communication. J. Med. Internet Res. **15**(4), e1933 (2013)
11. Rajpara, S., Botello, A., Townend, J., Ormerod, A.: Systematic review of dermoscopy and digital dermoscopy/artificial intelligence for the diagnosis of melanoma. Br. J. Dermatol. **161**(3), 591–604 (2009)
12. Shuvo, T.A., et al.: eHealth innovations in LMICs of Africa and Asia: a literature review exploring factors affecting implementation, scale-up, and sustainability. Health Care 8(9) (2015)
13. Sierra, C.H.: Corporeal transparency and biomedical imaging technologies: a new scientific imaginary of the gaze (2015)

14. Smailhodzic, E., Hooijsma, W., Boonstra, A., Langley, D.J.: Social media use in healthcare: a systematic review of effects on patients and on their relationship with healthcare professionals. BMC Health Serv. Res. **16**(1), 1–14 (2016)
15. Thomas, D.C., Arlene, C., Emilia, E., YXH, N.S.S.: The usage of cosmetic product containing skin-lightening ingredients among female nursing students in Sabah, Malaysia: a pre-liminary study. Malays. J. Med. Health Sci. **16**(105) (2020)
16. World Health Organization (WHO), et al.: African Region Health Report. United Nations, Geneva (2013)

User-Centered Design for Surgical Innovations: A Ventriculostomy Case Study

Jonatan Reyes[✉], Nadine El-Mufti, Shawn Gorman, David Xie, and Marta Kersten-Oertel

Department of Computer Science and Software Engineering, Gina Cody School of Engineering and Computer Science, Concordia University, Montréal, QC, Canada
j_yes@encs.concordia.ca

Abstract. A lack of multidisciplinary collaboration during the design phase of surgical innovation development often ignores the people whom we are developing for and therefore omits meaningful and relevant user insights that can potentially be gathered about the context-of-use of a product. To mitigate this issue, we propose a user-centered design approach to developing surgical solutions. End-user involvement during product design has been linked to the development of more useful and usable solutions as it helps create a smooth transition between research, environment, and daily practice. In this paper, we describe the user-centered design process and give an example of how it can be incorporated to enhance the development of surgical innovations. As a case study, we focus on one of the most commonly performed and error-prone neurosurgical procedures, ventriculostomy.

Keywords: UI/UX research · HCI · Design thinking · User-centered design · Ventriculostomy · Augmented Reality

1 Introduction

Research in surgical technologies has led to numerous novel hardware and software artifacts, e.g. deep learning methods for surgical video processing, augmented reality for surgical guidance, and robots/devices for minimally invasive surgery. Yet, only some of these innovations have met with success and have been incorporated into daily surgical practice. One reason for this, is the lack of multidisciplinary teams as well as the apparent mismatch between the technological and human needs [9]. Moreover, a lack of interdisciplinary research can result in a focus on either novel hardware use or algorithmic design rather than the needs of the intended end-user (e.g. surgeons) [27]. This has resulted in many proof-of-concept systems that have not been translated into clinical practice [14]. One way to address this is through the application of user-centered design (UCD) practices across areas of surgical innovation. UCD is an iterative design process

J. S. H. Baxter et al. (Eds.): EPIMI 2022/ML-CDS 2022/TDA4BiomedicalImaging 2022,
LNCS 13755, pp. 51–62, 2022.
https://doi.org/10.1007/978-3-031-23223-7_5

that focuses primarily on making systems more usable by prioritizing users, their activities, and contexts during each phase of a project.

When adopting a UCD approach, the first step of any clinical research would be to determine a practical problem or limitation of the end-user. Although perhaps obvious, this is not always possible, especially in academia. Generally, limited access to clinicians, operating rooms, and large cohorts of end users become common challenges. Moreover, trainees taking over existing projects miss out on the opportunity to work closely with clinicians and gaining first-hand experience, not to mention funding that can potentially end prior to rigorous clinical evaluation and validation of a system. These issues can drive researchers to end up solving problems that may not exist or ones that are inconsequential for medical professionals. Contrarily, the active participation of clinicians can ensure clinical relevance and promote feedback within an iterative user-centered design methodology that involves: research, analysis, brainstorming and analyzing ideas, getting feedback, improving a prototype, and testing. To date, however, design has played a limited role in surgical innovation research in academic centres despite the fact that it is well-suited for cross-disciplinary research.

In the following paper, we describe how a UCD approach can benefit surgical innovation projects. We begin with a description of the UCD design process. Then, present what this process could look like for the specific neurosurgical task of ventriculostomy. We conclude with a discussion about the importance of considering human aspects in the design process of clinical innovations, and point out the limitations of our study.

2 User-Centered Design

The term 'User-Centered Design' (UCD), coined by Donald Norman in the 1970's [18], is an iterative project-oriented dynamic design process that incorporates multidisciplinary expertise to meet user requirements and expectations while prioritizing ergonomics and product (hardware/software) usability. The adoption of a multidisciplinary collaborative design approach not only broadens a team's perspectives and skills, but also helps target a larger pool of users and puts them at the center of a product's design and development, leading to better outcomes and greater uptake [1]. While different variations of UCD exist, they all consist of three key principles: user involvement from the beginning, empirical measurement of product usage, and iterative design [2]. A typical UCD process has 5 stages: Research, Analysis, Design, Development, and Testing (Fig. 1). The 'disseminate' stage was included to account for the academic research model where knowledge transfer of the results is an important step to generate new ideas and future research directives [22].

A variety of **research** methods can be used to gather and leverage user insights to develop compelling user-centric products. Research includes: market research, observations, interviews and self-reported data, designer analysis and use case diagrams which provide a graphical depiction of a user's interaction with current products, etc. Combining findings from multiple sources and methods helps designers corroborate findings by minimizing inadequacies and

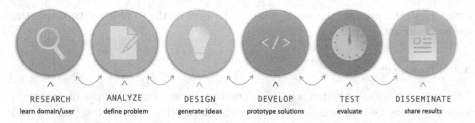

RESEARCH | ANALYZE | DESIGN | DEVELOP | TEST | DISSEMINATE
learn domain/user | define problem | generate ideas | prototype solutions | evaluate | share results

Fig. 1. User centered design is an iterative process with 5 main stages: Research, Analysis, Design, Development, and Testing (Figure). We add disseminate at the end of the UCD process to account for the academic research model.

increasing the validity and reliability of results. Once sufficient data has been collected, the goals, attitudes and behavioral patterns of the intended user can be deduced and **analyzed**. This helps designers gain a deeper understanding of their users' objectives and information needs, how they perform domain specific tasks and the system specifications required to accommodate these needs that result in concepts and designs that meet user and workflow requirements. After the problem(s) or limitation(s) have been clearly identified, the **design** step is used to generate ideas and tangible designs by incorporating information architecture, creating graphics, and designing user task flows to graphically depict the sequence of events that occur when a user performs a specific task. In order to facilitate the transition from design to **development**, a team must find a balance between design complexity and technical feasibility. Lastly, due to the continuous and dynamic nature of UCD lifecycles, **testing** generally occurs at the end of each design iteration where it serves as a quality check to validate whether the proposed solution successfully addresses specified user requirements and adheres to usability standards. As for evaluations, they are typically performed during the design and development stages and are carried out either heuristically by designers and experts or by end-users via usability testing to reveal and address a combination of different design problems. The former focuses on the compliance of a user interface (UI) with recognized usability principles whereas the latter evaluates the experience (UX) of a product by either testing it with potential users who are asked to perform tasks as they normally would while observers take notes or through the use of metrics to determine usability.

3   Case Study

In the following section, we go through a UCD design process in the context of ventriculostomy to illustrate its application as it relates to the development of surgical innovations. Ventriculostomy, one of the most common neurosurgical procedures ($24,380$/year in the US [26]), is an intervention that accesses the cerebrospinal fluid (CSF) pathways when these spaces are either enlarged or filled with blood, resulting in dangerous increases in intracranial pressure (ICP). The technique of ventriculostomy involves drilling a hole through the skull to the dura mater, and carefully guiding a silicone catheter, the external ventricular drain (EVD), through the brain tissue into one of the ventricles to drain the excess fluid and measure the pressure.

3.1 Research

The research process began with a literature review on the topic of ventriculostomy using Google scholar, the analysis of multimedia sources (videos and images), and a search for commercial ventriculostomy solutions. However, due to the pandemic and the resulting restrictions to emergency rooms (ERs), intensive-care units (ICUs), or operating rooms (ORs), we compensated and opted for alternative source of information, including watching videos of different techniques. After a comprehensive review of the literature (Fig. 2), we developed an interactive questionnaire[1] that was sent out to stakeholders.

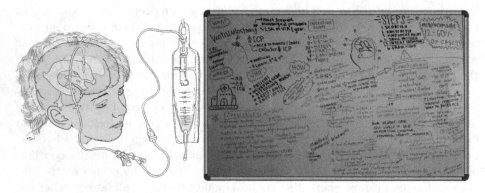

Fig. 2. Left: EVD schematic. **Right:** Whiteboard notes from discussion between HCI/design researchers, medical imaging experts, IGNS developers and engineers.

Procedure: The most common technique for EVD placement is by free-hand insertion. The main steps include: (1) general anesthesia; (2) selecting an entry point (i.e., Keen, Kocher, Dandy, Frazier, Kaufmann, or Tubbs' points, Kocher's frontal point being the most common), (3) local anesthesia, (4) making a small percutaneous incision, (5) drilling a hole through the skull to the dura mater, (6) opening the dura, and (7) guiding the EVD for a distance of about 5 cm, into the ventricles to drain the fluid and monitor the ICP. Whenever possible, pre-operative images, such as computed tomography (CT) or magnetic resonance imaging (MRI) scans, are used to visualize ventricle position, size, displacement, and relevant anatomy. The surgeon relies on external cranial anatomical landmarks to identify the ideal entry point and determine the best trajectory for safe drain placement. Due to cost, time, and equipment constraints, free-hand ventriculostomy is routinely the preferred choice [3]. Alternatives to free-hand cannulation include Ghajar guide-assisted cannulation (a physical guide),

---

[1] https://bit.ly/ucd-ventri.

endoscopic and image-guided neurosurgical (IGNS) systems. Only 3% of neuro-surgeons opt for Ghajar guides [13] due to their inability to account for mid-line shifts (the abnormal degeneration of the brain hemispheres caused by the pressure exerted from the buildup of blood and swelling [19,23]). Endoscopy is most often used in cases of hydrocephalus [25] and although IGNS systems show promise in determining the safest trajectory to target the ventricles with more precision [5], they are most commonly used in elective settings owing to their expensive, immobile/bulky, time-consuming nature, making them unsuitable for emergency situations [3].

Commercial Solutions: A number of intra-operative neuronavigation sys-tems are available on the market: StealthStation S8 Surgical Navigation Sys-tem (Medtronic, Minneapolis, USA), VectorVision neuronavigation (BrainLab, Munich, Germany) and Brainsight TMS Navigation, (BrainBox, Cardiff, United Kingdom). As for guiding/mechanical devices, the CODMAN ventriculostomy kit (Integra Lifesciences Corp., New Jersey, USA), and the Ghajar Guide Cra-nial Drill system (Neurodynamics Inc., New York, USA) are available. As for ultrasound-guidance, the Burr-Hole 8863 (BK Medical Holding Company, Inc., Massachusetts, USA), and the S31KP - Burr-Hole Guidance Transducer (Fuji-film, Massachusetts, USA) or (BK Medical, Denmark) can be used. Ultrasound-guided EVD uses a portable neurosurgical ultrasound scanner with a burr hole transducer as well as a single-use needle guide channel. Robotic-based systems, such as the "Evolution 1" (Universal Robots, Schwerin, Germany) uses a fixed and an articulated mobile platform (Physik Instrumente, Waldbronn, Germany) to assist EVD procedures. The major drawback of ultrasound-guided and robotic guided EVD is the need to enlarge the burr hole more than 13-mm-diameter. Further drawbacks of robot-assisted solutions are cost, configuration, and the extra space required for the hardware.

Research Systems: Many proof of concept systems have emerged in the area of neurosurgery, including mixed reality (augmented and virtual) [4], ultrasound-guided [24], robotic [29], and sonification assisted [20]. Augmented reality (AR) visualization superimpose pre-operative images and surgical plans directly onto the patient thus eliminate the continuous shift in focus between the patient and the IGNS system [15]. AR in ventriculostomy has been used to develop hap-tic simulation systems for resident students to practice catheter placement [28], interactive mixed-reality-based navigation systems to facilitate the targeting of the ventricles [4] as well as a visualization system using holograms of preop-erative CT-generated to guide the procedure [17]. Nevertheless, a number of shortcomings have been linked to AR use, including poor understanding of the depth/visuospatial perception of anatomical data, an inability to provide feed-back regarding precision or accuracy of registration, and/or the need to manually hold the AR device [7].

3.2   Analysis

Consistent with the literature, feedback from our survey's participants (from 5 neurosurgeons, 2 residents, 1 IGNS developer) describes the challenges and complications that prevent accurate EVD placement. In urgent settings, where acutely rising ICP mandates immediate ventricular access to stabilize ICP, targeting of the ventricle has been associated with up to 60% misplacement due to human error [21,23]. Based on the results of the questionnaire and reviews, we identified some of the factors that influenced these high rates, such as patient's age (i.e. neonates), abnormal anatomy (i.e. midline shifts, small ventricles), etymology of hydrocephalus (i.e., tumors, intracranial hemorrhage), bedside positioning, neurosurgeon's cognitive load, and lack of training/practice. Complications may included intracranial hemorrhage, midline shift, post-operative infection (i.e., meningitis, ventriculitis), technical/hardware failure (i.e., defective catheter), poor/inaccurate ICP measurements, no access to pre-operative imaging CT/MRI, CSF leakage, subdural CSF collection, seizures, inability to drain CSF, increase of cognitive load (i.e. when no guidance is used), communication delays, and gaps between disciplines [11,25]. All of these factors, in turn, can lead to increases in the length of hospital stays, morbidity and mortality [8].

After assessing the different challenges, we created a journey map[2] to describe a neurosurgeon's objectives, specific needs, and pain-points during ventriculostomy. Specifically, based on the results of our survey, we created the persona (archetype user) "Neurosurgeon Nancy", who works in a Canadian hospital and performs 1–2 EVD placements per week. Despite having access to IGNS systems, she always opts for freehand ventriculostomy as this is what she is most comfortable with. In addition, she has encountered all of the complications that were found in the literature, such as sub-optimal catheter placement, revisions, haemorrhage, and abnormal ventricular anatomy (i.e. midline shifts and small ventricles). Figure 3 outlines the different stages of interaction that Neurosurgeon Nancy goes through as they take place in her actual user environment; the resources, mechanisms or mediums of interaction; and the user's emotional state at each stage of the experience.

3.3   Design

This phase encourages the generation of solutions to improve the user's experience. Often, low-cost/low-effort designs are created (e.g., sketches, wireframes, mockups, and storyboards) in conjunction with risk components/processes that get tested in an experimental setting. Testing becomes an iterative process, aiming to align solutions with the ergonomic preferences and criteria of acceptance.

---

[2] A journey map is a tool used to illustrate the user's workflow, and cognitive load, while they are performing a specific task with the aim of identifying their main objectives and frustrations.

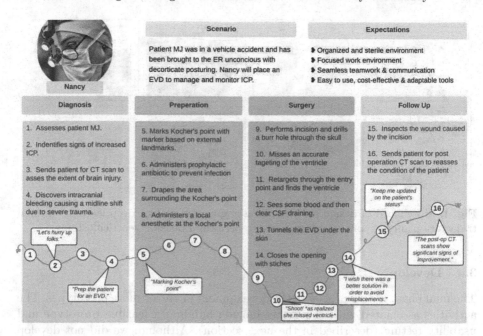

Fig. 3. Journey map of Neurosurgeon Nancy's main goals, frustrations, and specific needs while performing an urgent free-hand ventriculostomy. Dialog boxes express Nancy's thoughts and feelings at every stage of the scenario, and a trajectory line depicts the positive and negative moods.

Based on insights gathered from the questionnaire, primary users and their workflows, the authors of the paper had an ideation session where prospective solutions were identified. The focus was placed on key product design decisions for improving the targeting of the ventricles using a free-hand technique together with pre-operative images. Particular attention was paid to the use of tablets, mobile phones, and wearable devices for augmenting virtual images onto an anatomical space. Haptic feedback is considered as an alert mechanism to prevent damage to tissues/vessels. Other solutions considered included the use of sonification and deep learning to determine optimal trajectories.

Storyboards are visual aids used to communicate ideas of designs in a multidisciplinary team. In the context of product design, design teams use them to model user experiences and interactions with current or future products or services by using them as a medium of communication between team members and stakeholders [10]. They are used to detect a user's emotional engagement when performing a specific task. Figure 4 shows our storyboard, which narrates the flow of events from a normal to a problematic situation occurring in a fictitious ventriculostomy procedure and illustrates our vision of technological utility in clinical practice. In this story, Neurosurgeon Nancy and Resident Rakeem, perform a bedside procedure with the assistance of a mixed-reality solution.

Fig. 4. Storyboard of design solution using augmented reality, deep learning optimal trajectory planning, and sound guidance to perform a bedside ventriculostomy.

3.4   Develop

The final phase in this process is the development of one or more prototypes. The activities associated with this phase include building a feasible prototype and usability testing (described in the next section). Although we did not develop a functional prototype as it is beyond the scope of this paper, we nevertheless took on the task of aligning and validating prospective solutions with the acceptance criteria. To achieve this, we analyzed the results of our survey and found that 60% of the participants agreed that a sub-optimal catheter placement was a major complication of free-hand ventriculostomies. We also considered comments for improving the usability of our proposed solutions, such as "need something fast and accurate used in multiple settings" and "it needs to be introduced early in training and be easy to use and adaptable". We agreed that the introduction of novel technologies during training is essential as it can help facilitate the adoption and integration of technological artifacts into the operating room. Furthermore, we found that 50% of the responses were looking for cost-effective solutions to include in their daily practice. Therefore, based on these findings, we are encouraged to develop low-cost solutions that facilitate the localization of the ventricles with higher accuracy by leveraging intra-operative imaging and augmented reality for educational/training purposes as well as any of the applicable clinical settings (i.e. urgent, elective, emergent case).

We present two mock-ups that we designed based on the ideation session and survey responses. By leveraging the portability, affordability, and interactivity capabilities of tablets, our proposed system extends the MARIN system [16] for the projection of entry point, catheter trajectory and navigation to the target ventricles. Figure 5 (left) illustrates a mock-up of an AR tablet-based solution. With this solution, we combine gestures and anatomical landmarks to perform real-time manual registration between patients and virtual data (i.e. entry point, trajectories, and anatomical models). We envision the tablet being clamped to the patients bedside. Figure 5 (right) depicts a mockup of a mixed-reality solution using head-mounted displays. More specifically, we will utilize the ergonomic design, gestures, and visual capabilities of HoloLens II (Microsoft, Washington, USA) to enable similar tasks. Since combining sound and visual cues can reduce cognitive load in neurosurgery [20], we will integrate sound and color coding visualizations to assist with depth perception (e.g. changing color of catheter when on optimal trajectory). Haptic feedback is another way to explore depth perception and re-direct navigation.

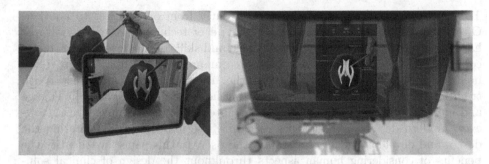

Fig. 5. Mock-ups of prospective augmented reality prototypes for users to evaluate in terms of design (UI) and usability (UX). **Left:** tablet and **Right:** head-mounted display solutions.

3.5   Test

The testing of a functional prototype is beyond the scope of this paper. However, from the beginning of the UCD process, we defined the requirements that our product will be evaluated against. Based on the results of our research, survey answers, and written and oral exchanges with neurosurgeons, we would consider the requirements of any ventriculostomy innovation: ease of use, easy to set-up, efficient, fast and accurate in multiple settings, adaptable, and cost effective. In addition, we would provide examples of evaluations for functional prototypes against the aforementioned requirements. As for the user study, we would ask participants to complete specific tasks while we observed their experience and document specific system's behaviors. For example, let's consider the following tasks: (1) allow surgeons to test the user interface of HoloLens, (2) perform registration/visualization of pre-operative imaging and anatomy, and (3) navigate to the target ventricle. Ideally, evaluations would be performed in the user's natural setting where the solution would normally be used (e.g. ICU).

Performance evaluations of these tasks would be based on objective and subjective success metrics. In our case study, we would measure, e.g., set-up time, the number of interactions performed, accuracy in catheter placement, and execution time. We would also conduct subjective assessments to measure the robustness of visualization, aesthetics of user-interface, cognitive load, attention, and overall user experience. To achieve this, we would utilize Think Aloud, an assessment tool where users thoughts and actions are recorded while performing a task; the System Usability Scale (SUS) [6] a subjective assessment tool that measures usability and user satisfaction; and the NASA Task Load Index (TLX) [12], which rates perceived workload while performing a task or immediately afterwards. After testing a number of different prototypes, a clinical trial would generally take place using the finalized system.

4 Discussion

Technology development strategies vary greatly from one project to another. Often the design choices depend on the type of technology (i.e., software or hardware), development tools available, size and skills of the development team, complexity of the project, budget, risks, communication/feedback from stakeholders, and certain assumption about the usage of the final product. With traditional development approaches realizing how end-users will actually engage and interact with the product often comes late in the development cycle. However, modern design methodologies recognize the importance of centering the design and development process around the user. In this paper, we identify the benefits of considering human aspects throughout the design of clinical solutions. We also show that a user-centered approach is valuable when designing and developing technologies in the clinical domain.

There are a number of limitations of this study that deserve to be mentioned. Despite the efforts made to disseminate the survey through different mediums, we only collected responses from people affiliated with medical centers in Canada, US, Mexico, and Guatemala. Therefore, the user and workflow requirements as well as the design decisions proposed in this study are biased towards western nations. Furthermore, to date we have a limited number of responses (8), with zero responses from certain stakeholders (e.g. anesthetists, nurses, and practitioners).

5 Conclusion

Next-generation surgical tools, coupled with advancements in hardware, medical imaging, virtual and augmented reality, and artificial intelligence, are profoundly impacting healthcare with improvements in patient care, quality, and safety of surgical procedures. However, their adoption into clinical workflows and daily practice has been slow, or even disregarded, due to an inadequate understanding of the primary users, usage, ergonomics, and other pragmatic considerations often overlooked during their development.

With this ventriculostomy case study, our aim was to demonstrate the steps needed to drive the development of successful surgical solutions using a user-centered design approach. Furthermore, we highlight the importance of multidisciplinary collaboration and how it can generate efficient, explainable, and usable solutions based on acceptance criteria stipulated by the persons intended to use them. With the user validating the solution at every step of the development cycle, a strong sense of trust can be built before the novelty is accepted into practice. One key advantage of using an iterative design process is that communication becomes an integral part of the design by making concepts and ideas tangible and thus accessible to all disciplines and users for discussion and evaluation. Such discussion and feedback are necessary for evaluating new technologies and providing evidence of their benefits. We believe that design will eventually take a more prominent role in the development of surgical tools and technologies and will be the driving force behind pushing innovations from laboratory to clinic.

References

1. Chammas, A., Quaresma, M., Mont'Alvão, C.: A closer look on the user centred design. Proc. Manuf. **3**, 5397–5404 (2015). 6th International Conference on Applied Human Factors and Ergonomics (AHFE 2015) and the Affiliated Conferences, AHFE 2015
2. Introduction to user experience. In: Baxter, K., Courage, C., Caine, K. (eds.) Understanding Your Users. Interactive Technologies, 2nd edn., pp. 2–20. Morgan Kaufmann, Boston (2015)
3. Amoo, M., Henry, J., Javadpour, M.: Common trajectories for freehand frontal ventriculostomy: a systematic review. World Neurosurg. **146**, 292–297 (2021)
4. Ansari, N., Léger, É., Kersten-Oertel, M.: VentroAR: augmented reality platform for ventriculostomy using the Microsoft hololens. Accepted to Augmented Environments in Computer Assisted Interventions Special Issue of Computer Methods in Biomechanics and Biomedical Engineering: Imaging & Visualization (2022)
5. Broggi, G., Dones, I., Ferroli, P., Franzini, A., Servello, D., Duca, S.: Image guided neuroendoscopy for third ventriculostomy. Acta Neurochir. **142**(8), 893–899 (2000)
6. Brooke, J., et al.: SUS-a quick and dirty usability scale. Usabil. Eval. Ind. **189**(194), 4–7 (1996)
7. Cho, J., Rahimpour, S., Cutler, A., Goodwin, C.R., Lad, S.P., Codd, P.: Enhancing reality: a systematic review of augmented reality in neuronavigation and education. World Neurosurg. **139**, 186–195 (2020)
8. Edwards, N.C., Engelhart, L., Casamento, E.M., McGirt, M.J.: Cost-consequence analysis of antibiotic-impregnated shunts and external ventricular drains in hydrocephalus. J. Neurosurg. **122**(1), 139–147 (2015)
9. Freudenthal, A., Stüdeli, T., Lamata, P., Samset, E.: Collaborative co-design of emerging multi-technologies for surgery. J. Biomed. Inform. **44**(2), 198–215 (2011)
10. Haesen, M., Meskens, J., Luyten, K., Coninx, K.: Supporting multidisciplinary teams and early design stages using storyboards. In: Jacko, J.A. (ed.) HCI 2009. LNCS, vol. 5610, pp. 616–623. Springer, Heidelberg (2009). https://doi.org/10.1007/978-3-642-02574-7_69
11. Hagel, S., Bruns, T., Pletz, M., Engel, C., Kalff, R., Ewald, C.: External ventricular drain infections: risk factors and outcome. Interdisc. Perspect. Infect. Diseases **2014** (2014)
12. Hart, S.G.: Nasa-task load index (NASA-TLX); 20 years later. In: Proceedings of the Human Factors and Ergonomics Society Annual Meeting, vol. 50, pp. 904–908. Sage Publications, Los Angeles (2006)
13. Huyette, D.R., Turnbow, B.J., Kaufman, C., Vaslow, D.F., Whiting, B.B., Oh, M.Y.: Accuracy of the freehand pass technique for ventriculostomy catheter placement: retrospective assessment using computed tomography scans. J. Neurosurg. **108**(1), 88–91 (2008)

14. Kersten-Oertel, M., Jannin, P., Collins, D.L.: The state of the art of visualization in mixed reality image guided surgery. Comput. Med. Imaging Graph. **37**(2), 98–112 (2013)
15. Léger, É., Drouin, S., Collins, D.L., Popa, T., Kersten-Oertel, M.: Quantifying attention shifts in augmented reality image-guided neurosurgery. Healthc. Technol. Lett. **4**(5), 188–192 (2017)
16. Léger, É., et al.: MARIN: an open-source mobile augmented reality interactive neuronavigation system. Int. J. Comput. Assist. Radiol. Surg. **15**(6), 1013–1021 (2020)
17. Li, Y., et al.: A wearable mixed-reality holographic computer for guiding external ventricular drain insertion at the bedside. J. Neurosurg. **131**(5), 1599–1606 (2018)
18. Mithun, A.M., Mithun, A.M., Yafooz, W.M.S.: Extended user centered design (UCD) process in the aspect of human computer interaction. In: 2018 International Conference on Smart Computing and Electronic Enterprise (ICSCEE), pp. 1–6 (2018)
19. Paramore, C., Turner, D.: Relative risks of ventriculostomy infection and morbidity. Acta Neurochir. **127**(1), 79–84 (1994)
20. Plazak, J., DiGiovanni, D.A., Collins, D.L., Kersten-Oertel, M.: Cognitive load associations when utilizing auditory display within image-guided neurosurgery. Int. J. Comput. Assist. Radiol. Surg. **14**(8), 1431–1438 (2019). https://doi.org/10.1007/s11548-019-01970-w
21. Raabe, C., Fichtner, J., Beck, J., Gralla, J., Raabe, A.: Revisiting the rules for freehand ventriculostomy: a virtual reality analysis. J. Neurosurg. **128**(4), 1250–1257 (2018)
22. Raidou, R.G., Furmanová, K., Grossmann, N., Casares-Magaz, O., et al.: Lessons learnt from developing visual analytics applications for adaptive prostate cancer radiotherapy. In: VisGap–The Gap between Visualization Research and Visualization Software, pp. 51–58. The Eurographics Association (2020)
23. Rehman, T., et al.: A us-based survey on ventriculostomy practices. Clin. Neurol. Neurosurg. **114**(6), 651–654 (2012)
24. Rieger, A., Rainov, N., Sanchin, L., Schöpp, G., Burkert, W.: Ultrasound-guided endoscopic fenestration of the third ventricular floor for non-communicating hydrocephalus. min-Minimally Invasive Neurosurg. **39**(01), 17–20 (1996)
25. Sacko, O., Boetto, S., Lauwers-Cances, V., Dupuy, M., Roux, F.E.: Endoscopic third ventriculostomy: outcome analysis in 368 procedures. J. Neurosurg. Pediatr. **5**(1), 68–74 (2010)
26. Sekula, R., Cohen, D., Patek, P., Jannetta, P., Oh, M.: Epidemiology of ventriculostomy in the united states from 1997 to 2001. Br. J. Neurosurg. **22**(2), 213–218 (2008)
27. Trudel, C.M.: Useful, usable and used? In: Recent Advances in Technologies for Inclusive Well-Being, pp. 43–63 (2021)
28. Yudkowsky, R., et al.: Practice on an augmented reality/haptic simulator and library of virtual brains improves residents' ability to perform a ventriculostomy. Simul. Healthc. **8**(1), 25–31 (2013)
29. Zimmermann, M., Krishnan, R., Raabe, A., Seifert, V.: Robot-assisted navigated endoscopic ventriculostomy: implementation of a new technology and first clinical results. Acta Neurochir. **146**(7), 697–704 (2004)

Multimodal Learning and Fusion Across Scales for Clinical Decision Support

Visually Aware Metadata-Guided Supervision for Improved Skin Lesion Classification Using Deep Learning

Anshul Pundhir[✉] [iD], Ananya Agarwal[iD], Saurabh Dadhich[iD],
and Balasubramanian Raman[iD]

Indian Institute of Technology, Roorkee, Roorkee, India
{anshul_p,bala}@cs.iitr.ac.in, ananya_a@ch.iitr.ac.in,
saurabh_d@mt.iitr.ac.in

Abstract. Nowadays, skin cancer has become a common disease and is growing worldwide at an increasing rate. Its manual examination by dermatologists demands significant time and cost in terms of instruments. Also, practical diagnosis demands experienced and skilled dermatologists. These challenges show the impracticality of manual diagnosis over the increased rate of skin cancer patients and thus demand robust end-to-end computer-aided diagnosis (CAD) methods. This paper proposes a deep learning-based skin lesion classification approach that utilizes the visual attention-based mechanism over Convolutional Neural Networks (CNNs) to improve visual context. We use the information from skin lesion images and patient demographics to enhance visual attention, which further improves classification. The proposed method accurately classifies deadly melanoma skin cancer for the PAD-UFES-20 dataset, an essential but challenging task. Our proposed approach has been evaluated over multimodel data, i.e., clinical and dermoscopic images, using two publicly available datasets named PAD-UFES-20 and ISIC-2019. During experimentation, our approach surpasses the available state-of-the-art techniques over five commonly used Convolutional Neural Networks (CNNs) architectures which validate its generalizability and applicability in different scenarios. Our approach achieved efficient performance for small datasets like PAD-UFES-20 using a lightweight model (MobileNet), making it suitable for the CAD system. The effectiveness of our method has been shown by various quantitative and qualitative measures, which demonstrate its efficacy in addressing challenging lesion diagnoses. Our source code is publicly available to reproduce the work.

Keywords: Multimodal fusion · Computer-aided diagnosis · Attention mechanism

1 Introduction

Skin cancer has become a common cancer type; one in every three cancers diagnosed is a skin cancer [30]. Skin cancer mainly occurs due to exposure to harmful

---

A. Pundhir, A. Agarwal and S. Dadhich—Equal Contribution.

© The Author(s), under exclusive license to Springer Nature Switzerland AG 2022
J. S. H. Baxter et al. (Eds.): EPIMI 2022/ML-CDS 2022/TDA4BiomedicalImaging 2022,
LNCS 13755, pp. 65–76, 2022.
https://doi.org/10.1007/978-3-031-23223-7_6

radiation from the sun that damages the skin and causes cell mutations. Skin cancer is mainly categorized into three categories- Basal Cell Carcinoma (BCC), Squamous Cell Carcinoma (SCC), and Melanoma [23]. Out of these three categories, BCC and SCC represents major skin cancer cases but involve lower risks due to lesser metastasize. Among these skin cancer classes, melanoma is the deadliest skin-cancer type due to its high metastasis rate, but also the rarest. Fortunately, melanoma can be treatable if detected in the early stage [19]. Skin lesion conditions are inspected visually with the help of a dermatoscope that enables dermatologists to analyze the morphological features related to skin tissues which are not feasible to visualize with naked eyes. Dermatoscopy is a non-invasive technique, but it requires skilled dermatologists, huge manual efforts, and significant time to examine skin lesions carefully. Moreover, dermatoscope is costly and not easily available in developing countries, limiting skin lesion diagnosis.

To address these challenges, there is a critical need to develop computer-aided-diagnosis methods to perform skin lesion classification automatically. Past research has proven the benefits of leveraging deep-learning-based models like CNNs to perform medical imaging-related tasks like segmentation and classification [7,8,22]. Codella et al. [10], Steva et al. [13], Yu et al. [31] achieved notable improvement by applying CNNs. In recent studies, Deep Neural Networks (DNNs) have been found capable of attaining dermatologist-level performance [1,6]. Such findings motivate the applicability and development of CAD-based approaches. In practical scenarios during skin lesion analysis, dermatologists also consider the patients' demographics, i.e., skin type, body part, age, gender, etc., for final prediction. This fact supports the significance of clinical features for our use case, i.e., multi-modal fusion by using textual information with images. Information fusion helps to enrich features and henceforth improve the capability of DNNs by utilizing complementary information [5]. Arroyo et al. [4], Lin et al. [20], and Liu et al. [21] used CNN-based ensemble approaches to fuse visual information obtained through various CNNs, but such approaches are computationally expensive.

Some notable contributions toward skin lesion classification using feature fusion have been made by Liu et al. [2], Pacheco and Krohling [23], and Kharazmin et al. [18]. These approaches seem to lack the full potential to utilize the significance of clinical information during fusion. To address the above issues, Li et al. [19] and Pacheco and Krohling [24] proposed different fusion approaches for further improvements. These approaches lack in utilizing multi-level visual contextual information concerning the skin lesion. So, there is scope for a better fusion approach for further improvements while fusing patients' demographics with image-based features.

We have utilized the clinical and dermoscopy images, which shows the generalizability of our approach to different image modalities. Moreover, clinical-image-based CAD can be easily adopted since such images can be readily captured using smartphone cameras compared to dermoscopy images. In the proposed work, we improved the visual feature maps with the help of an attention mechanism [17] while extracting features with the help of convolutional neural networks. Moreover, we have used available patients' demographics for further supervising the obtained features. Our work is evaluated on clinical as well as dermoscopy images using two publicly available datasets named PAD-UFES-20 [3] and ISIC-19 [9,11,16,29] and outperforms available state-of-the-art approaches [19,23,24] over five CNNs. The robustness of our method to address challenging lesion categories has been proven using several quantitative and qualitative measures. Our contribution is summarized as follows:

- We demonstrated the impact of considering the patients' demographics in improving skin lesion classification. During the ablation study, we found huge classification improvement for the PAD-UFES dataset, which is relatively small but contains enough clinical information. This improvement proves the utility of the proposed work toward the applicability of deep learning models for smaller datasets with clinical information.
- To the best of our knowledge, we are the first one to re-purpose the idea of visual attention in combination with meta-features or patient clinical information to guide and enhance the feature representation to improve the classification rate. Moreover, the proposed approach accurately classifies melanoma (without any error) over the PAD-UFES-20 dataset using ResNet50 architecture.
- During experimentation, our idea of concatenating global meta supervision with attentive local features yields robust feature representation due to the alignment of local visual context to global visual feature representation and meta-guided global feature set.
- During ablation, we have proved that the idea of concatenating global context to attentive local features gives a better feature set, i.e., the combination of only attentive local features is not enough to represent the visual features completely.
- The proposed end-to-end framework generalizes over five CNNs and multimodal datasets (clinical and dermoscopy images), and their effectiveness has been validated quantitatively and qualitatively.

The remaining paper is organized as follows: The proposed approach is explained in Sect. 2; Experiments conducted to develop the approach have been elaborated in Sect. 3. Finally, Discussion and Conclusions with future scope have been drawn in Sect. 4 and Sect. 5 respectively.

2   Proposed Method

This section describes the intuition and methodology of the proposed approach, as shown in Fig. 1. Fundamentally, our approach tries to mimic the skin-diagnostic procedure. During visual inspection, dermatologists focus on the skin lesion, and the patients' demographics assist in the final decision. To enhance visual inspection, we utilized the visual attention mechanism to CNNs inspired by [17] and improved it further by incorporating global visual context. We fuse the patients' demographics with the visual information for final assistance. The proposed end-to-end approach mainly consists of a Visual Feature Extraction Module, Meta Feature Extraction Module, Visual Attention Module, Global Meta-Fusion Module, and Classification Module.

2.1 Problem Formulation

Assume set of skin lesion images (X_{img}) and patients' demographics (X_{info}) (also known as clinical or meta information) be the features and skin lesion types be the class label y such that $y \in \{1, 2, ..., N_{class}\}$, where N_{class} denotes the number of skin lesion categories. Then, we can represent our skin lesion classification problem as $\{X_{img}, X_{info}, y\}$ with the objective of predicting class label y using set of features $\{X_{img}, X_{info}\}$.

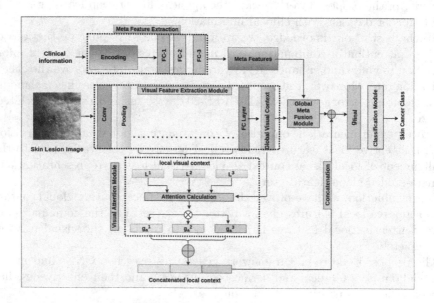

Fig. 1. Schematic architecture of the proposed approach.

2.2 Visual Feature Extraction Module

This module contains the CNN which acts as the visual feature extractor ϕ^k_{img} to extract visual features at layer k from the given set of images X_{img} as shown by Eq. 1.

$$f^k_{img} = \phi^k_{img}(X_{img}) \tag{1}$$

where, visual features, $f^k_{img} \in \mathbb{R}^{c_{img} \times h_{img} \times w_{img}}$, and c_{img} represents number of feature maps having shape $h_{img} \times w_{img}$. Here, f^k_{img} represent the visual features/visual context obtained at layers k by using visual feature extractor ϕ^k. At the final layer of a CNN, f^k_{img} denotes the feature vector, i.e., fully connected layer, while at intermediate layers, it denotes the visual feature maps.

2.3   Meta Feature Extraction Module

Firstly, this module encoded the patients' meta information X_{info} by following one hot-encoding, where missing information is filled with zero. After encoding, we obtained encoded meta information $X'_{info} \in \mathbb{R}^{\,d_{meta}}$, where d_{meta} denotes the dimension of encoded meta information. This one-hot encoded metadata is processed using three layer fully connected neural networks to get meta features f_{meta} where $f_{meta} \in \mathbb{R}^{\,g_{img}}$, where g_{img} denotes the dimension of global visual context.

2.4   Visual Attention Module

This module helps refine the visual information and supports our model to focus on the area of interest (skin lesion). To achieve this, we utilize an attention mechanism that helps to measure the similarity between local visual context L and global visual context g. Global visual context lies in the final feature layer of any CNN, while local visual context resides in intermediate layers. First, we have increased the number of channels in the local context, L, by using 1×1 convolutions to equate with the number of channels in g. We denote the local context of any given layer k as $L^k = \{l_1{}^k, l_2{}^k, ..., l_n{}^k\}$ where each $l_i{}^k$ denotes the activations at the given spatial location i of L^k. We have projected g to order of $1 \times 1 \times c\_img$ using adaptive average pooling.

We utilize the dot product to measure the similarity between g and given l_i for i^{th} spatial location in terms of compatibility scores, c_i using Eq. 2. The compatibility score reflects the degree of similarity between the given spatial location of the local context with respect to the global context. The compatibility score for given layer k is normalized by softmax using Eq. 3.

Please note that the value of k (i.e., the number of local context layers to consider) and the position for intermediate local context layers are inspired by the idea proposed by Saumya et al. [17]. Moreover, we have chosen the CNN layers (i.e., intermediate layers), which are closer to the global feature vector since the initial CNN layers represent the low-level features (which are less similar to the global context). For this work, our motivation is to show the impact of considering visual attention to improve the classification rate during skin lesion analysis. However, the number and position of intermediate layers required to represent the global context as a linear combination of local context also depend on the CNN considered, which opens the scope for future research.

$$c_i{}^k = <l_i{}^k, g> \tag{2}$$

$$a_i{}^k = \frac{exp(c_i{}^k)}{\sum_{j=1}^{n} exp(c_j{}^k)} \tag{3}$$

$A^k = \{a_1{}^k, a_2{}^k, ..., a_n{}^k\}$, denotes the normalized compatibility score for layer k. Finally, to align the local context L^k with global context g, we performed element wise weighted summation as $g_a{}^k = \sum_{i=1}^{n} a_i{}^k \cdot l_i{}^k$, where $g_a{}^k$ denotes attentive local features for the layer k aligned with respect to global visual context.

2.5   Global Meta Fusion Module

This modules helps to guide the global context, g with f_{meta} i.e. meta features obtained from patients' demographics. Global context g is fused with f_{meta} using Eq. 4.

$$g_{meta} = g \odot f_{meta} \qquad (4)$$

where g_{meta} denotes the meta-guided global context or global meta context, and $\odot$ denotes element-wise multiplication operation. Please note that we have used global context g (not global meta context g_{meta}) for calculating the attentive local features $g_a{}^k$. Since meta-information (after fusing with global context g) will change the visual global semantic information, making it less suitable to align local context with actual global visual context. Moreover, for calculating g_{meta}, we do not use feature concatenation because it fails to model the feature relationship during multi-modal fusion [19].

2.6   Classification Module

Finally, we take the k attentive local features, $\{g_a{}^1, g_a{}^2 ...., g_a{}^k\}$ computed in intermediate layers and fuse it with global meta context g_{meta} through feature concatenation to form the global feature vector g_{final} using Eq. 5.

$$g_{final} = [g_a{}^1, g_a{}^2 ...., g_a{}^k, g_{meta}] \qquad (5)$$

Our intuition to decide the location and number of local contexts is inspired by [17]. In this way, we refine our local visual context so that the model pays attention to spatial locations covering the lesion locations. The classification module takes the global feature vector g_{final} as input and classifies the skin lesion category.

3   Experiments and Results

This section elaborates on our experimental setup and performance evaluation over two benchmark datasets named PAD-UFES-20 and ISIC-2019. We trained five CNNs and surpassed current state-of-the-art (SOTA) performance.

3.1   Datasets

PAD-UFES-20 dataset contains 2,298 clinical skin lesion images captured using smartphone devices. This dataset covers six lesion categories with 21 patient clinical details like gender, age, cancer history, etc. Skin lesion categories include Basal Cell Carcinoma, Melanoma, Squamous Cell Carcinoma, Actinic Keratosis, Nevus, and Seborrheic Keratosis. ISIC-19 is a large dataset containing 25,331 training and 8238 test dermoscopy images with three clinical features: age, anatomical location, and gender. This dataset covers eight skin lesion categories: Melanocytic Nevus, Actinic Keratosis, Dermatofibroma, Squamous Cell Carcinoma, Melanoma, Basal Cell Carcinoma, Benign Keratosis, and Vascular Lesion. For experimentation, we have used the training dataset split images from ISIC-19 as ground truths for test split images are private.

3.2 Implementation Details

The experiments have been carried out on Ubuntu 20.04 and implemented using the PyTorch programming framework. Models are trained and evaluated on the NVIDIA Quadro P5000 workstation with 16 GB graphics memory. The proposed approach is compared with other approaches using five CNN architectures, i.e., MobileNet-V2 [26], DenseNet-121 [15], EfficientNet-B4 [28], VGG-13 [27], and ResNet50 [14]. We have followed the train-test split of 80:20 for PAD-UFES-20 and ISIC-19 datasets. For the ISIC-19 dataset, we considered the publicly available images to train and evaluate our model since ground truths for test data are unavailable. During experimentation, CNNs are loaded with pre-trained ImageNet [12] weights, and further fine-tuned on PAD-UFES-20 and ISIC-19 datasets over 150 epochs. Weighted cross-entropy loss is used to address the issue of imbalanced classes, where weight is inversely proportional to the number of instances present in the given class. While training our models, we used the SGD optimizer with a learning rate of 0.001 and a stepLR scheduler having a step size of 20. For further related details, we have made our source code publicly available to reproduce our work[1].

3.3 Ablation Study

We conducted an ablation study to analyze the impact of different modules on the overall performance, which helped to decide the overall architecture of the proposed approach. We performed experimentation on both datasets with ResNet50 as the baseline model during ablation. Firstly, we incorporated the visual attention module with intermediate local feature maps from the baseline architecture, named as **attn**. Secondly, we fused the global feature vector with the attentive local features using feature concatenation, named as **attn + g_c**. The improvement found in **attn + g_c** shows that the linear combination of attentive local features is not enough to represent the global context completely, so considering the global feature vector further helps improve performance. Finally, we guided the global visual features with the processed meta-features using the element-wise multiplication method (as explained in Sect. 2.5). We then fused the meta-guided global features with the attentive local features through feature concatenation, named as **attn + g_c + meta**. From Table 1, we found progressive improvement in the classification accuracy. So, we decided the architecture of **attn + g_c + meta** as our proposed approach. Please note that, we have not experimented for variation **g_c + meta** (i.e., fusion of meta-information with the global visual context) as it leads towards the prior work MetaNet [19] which has been outperformed by the proposed approach (as shown in Table 2 and Table 3).

---

[1] https://github.com/AnshulPundhir/VisualMetaGuidedSkinLesionClassification.

Table 1. Ablation study using ResNet50. Each value denotes the accuracy (ACC) obtained.

Dataset	Baseline	attn	attn + g_c	attn + g_c + meta
PAD-UFES-20	0.616	0.671	0.692	**0.812**
ISIC-19	0.767	0.772	0.812	**0.827**

3.4 Comparison with Other Methods

We compared our approach with three different techniques using five CNN architectures on PAD-UFES-20 and ISIC-2019 datasets. This comparison is shown using accuracy (ACC), balanced accuracy (BACC) and area under curve (AUC) [25] and summarized in Table 2 and Table 3. Balanced accuracy (BACC) is considered the main metric for fair comparison over the imbalanced dataset. To save computational time, we reuse the performance measures for these approaches over different CNNs as reported by [24]. The proposed method outperformed the available state-of-the-art (SOTA) techniques for every CNN considered. Please note that we have not compared our results with ISIC-19 winners since they considered "unknown" skin lesion classes also, which limits our comparison with previous approaches (Concatenation [23], MetaNet [19], and MetaBlock [24]) as they considered "known" skin lesion classes only because the handling of "unknown" classes is beyond the scope of the paper and require additional techniques).

4 Discussion

This section summarizes the insights obtained while analyzing the results. From the ablation study (Table 1), we realized the importance of visual attention in focusing on relevant regions of the lesion. Also, we have demonstrated the benefits of considering the global feature vector to improve the overall visually attentive feature representation. We computed global meta context to provide meta-information assistance, which significantly improves performance. Table 2 and Table 3 affirm the reliability and effectiveness of the approach over different imaging modalities and CNNs. Moreover, the proposed approach significantly improved performance over the PAD-UFES-20 dataset, containing only 2298 images with richer clinical information. This verifies the utility of the proposed method in effectively utilizing clinical data to guide the overall prediction where the dataset size is small. However, in Table 1, the relative improvement for ISIC-19 is smaller than PAD-UEES-20 due to very less patient clinical information available in ISIC-19. The Melanoma classification is challenging due to its rareness and limited instances. Still, during class-wise prediction (Fig. 2), our model classifies melanoma (deadliest skin cancer) with 100% accuracy using ResNet50 over PAD-UFES-20. Since BCC and SCC lesions are visually alike and pigmented, dermatologists face difficulties predicting them. Still, our model

Table 2. Comparison on PAD-UFES-20.

Model	ACC	BACC	AUC
Concatenation [23]			
MobileNet-V2	0.738	0.741	0.927
VGGNet-13	0.712	0.72	0.929
ResNet-50	0.741	0.728	0.929
EfficientNet-B4	0.765	0.758	0.945
DenseNet-121	0.742	0.747	0.932
MetaNet [19]			
MobileNet-V2	0.700	0.717	0.922
VGGNet-13	0.749	0.754	0.937
ResNet-50	0.732	0.742	0.936
EfficientNet-B4	0.744	0.737	0.931
DenseNet-121	0.745	0.745	0.932
MetaBlock [24]			
MobileNet-V2	0.724	0.754	0.938
VGGNet-13	0.728	0.736	0.933
ResNet-50	0.735	0.765	0.935
EfficientNet-B4	0.748	0.77	0.944
DenseNet-121	0.723	0.746	0.931
Proposed approach			
MobileNet-V2	0.806	**0.789**	0.954
VGGNet-13	0.807	**0.77**	0.952
ResNet-50	0.812	**0.806**	0.953
EfficientNet-B4	0.772	**0.784**	0.953
DenseNet-121	0.799	**0.779**	0.950

Table 3. Comparison on ISIC-19.

Model	ACC	BACC	AUC
Concatenation [23]			
MobileNet-V2	0.716	0.723	0.946
VGGNet-13	0.724	0.729	0.949
ResNet-50	0.729	0.726	0.948
EfficientNet-B4	0.784	0.768	0.96
DenseNet-121	0.738	0.737	0.952
MetaNet [19]			
MobileNet-V2	0.742	0.731	0.955
VGGNet-13	0.767	0.746	0.959
ResNet-50	0.753	0.746	0.956
EfficientNet-B4	0.766	0.756	0.959
DenseNet-121	0.725	0.723	0.949
MetaBlock [24]			
MobileNet-V2	0.777	0.760	0.958
VGGNet-13	0.753	0.74	0.955
ResNet-50	0.804	0.771	0.966
EfficientNet-B4	0.807	0.762	0.962
DenseNet-121	0.800	0.769	0.965
Proposed approach			
MobileNet-V2	0.804	**0.79**	0.968
VGGNet-13	0.846	**0.818**	0.976
ResNet-50	0.827	**0.791**	0.971
EfficientNet-B4	0.826	**0.782**	0.968
DenseNet-121	0.839	**0.807**	0.967

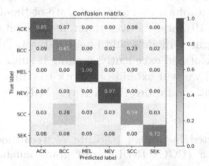
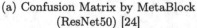

(a) Confusion Matrix by MetaBlock (ResNet50) [24]

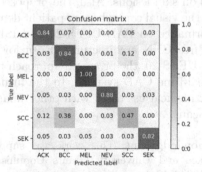

(b) Confusion Matrix by Proposed Approach (ResNet50)

Fig. 2. Overall improvement by proposed approach for categorical classification using PAD-UFES-20.

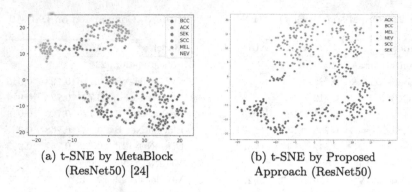

(a) t-SNE by MetaBlock
(ResNet50) [24]

(b) t-SNE by Proposed
Approach (ResNet50)

Fig. 3. t-SNE based comparision.

classifies BCC with an improvement of 19% over metablock. However, misclassifications (SCC vs. BCC) open scope for future improvement. But, this is not much of a problem as both are cancerous and require biopsy. Our approach has improved class-wise performance by 7% in comparison to metablock [24]. In Fig. 3, we have shown t-SNE visualization to compare how well-separated clusters have been obtained by our approach. Please note that we have used ResNet50 over PAD-UFES-20 to provide a fair comparison since MetaBlock achieves the best results on this configuration.

5   Conclusion and Future Work

We propose an inspired behavioral mechanism that mimics dermatologists' diagnostic behavior for the first time. To achieve this, we improved visual attention to focus on skin lesions. Also, the proposed meta fusion strategy effectively supervises the visual context using patient demographics' and achieved state-of-the-art performance on PAD-UFES-20 and ISIC-19 datasets over different modalities with five CNN architectures. Even for lighter models and small datasets like PAD-UFES-20, the proposed approach performed excellently, making it suitable for real-time CAD systems. In the future, we will extend our work to enhance other medical use-cases with other imaging modalities like X-Rays, MRIs, and CT Scans.

Acknowledgment. This work was supported by Indian Institute of Technology Roorkee and University Grants Commission (UGC) INDIA with grant number: 190510040512.

References

1. Haenssle, H.A., et al.: Man against machine: diagnostic performance of a deep learning convolutional neural network for dermoscopic melanoma recognition in comparison to 58 dermatologists. Ann. Oncol. **29**(8), 1836–1842 (2018)

2. Liu, Y., et al.: A deep learning system for differential diagnosis of skin diseases. Nat. Med. **26**(6), 900–908 (2020)
3. Pacheco, A.G., et al.: PAD-UFES-20: a skin lesion dataset composed of patient data and clinical images collected from smartphones. Data Brief **32**, 106221 (2020)
4. Arroyo, R., Alcantarilla, P.F., Bergasa, L.M., Romera, E.: Fusion and binarization of CNN features for robust topological localization across seasons. In: 2016 IEEE/RSJ International Conference on Intelligent Robots and Systems (IROS), pp. 4656–4663. IEEE (2016)
5. Atrey, P.K., Hossain, M.A., El Saddik, A., Kankanhalli, M.S.: Multimodal fusion for multimedia analysis: a survey. Multimed. Syst. **16**(6), 345–379 (2010)
6. Brinker, T.J., et al.: Deep learning outperformed 136 of 157 dermatologists in a head-to-head dermoscopic melanoma image classification task. Eur. J. Cancer **113**, 47–54 (2019)
7. Brinker, T.J., et al.: Skin cancer classification using convolutional neural networks: systematic review. J. Med. Internet Res. **20**(10), e11936 (2018)
8. Celebi, M.E., Codella, N., Halpern, A.: Dermoscopy image analysis: overview and future directions. IEEE J. Biomed. Health Inform. **23**(2), 474–478 (2019)
9. Codella, N.C., et al.: Skin lesion analysis toward melanoma detection: a challenge at the 2017 international symposium on biomedical imaging (ISBI), hosted by the international skin imaging collaboration (ISIC). In: 2018 IEEE 15th International Symposium on Biomedical Imaging (ISBI 2018), pp. 168–172. IEEE (2018)
10. Codella, N.C., et al.: Deep learning ensembles for melanoma recognition in dermoscopy images. IBM J. Res. Dev. **61**(4/5), 5-1 (2017)
11. Combalia, M., et al.: BCN20000: dermoscopic lesions in the wild. arXiv preprint arXiv:1908.02288 (2019)
12. Deng, J., Dong, W., Socher, R., Li, L.J., Li, K., Fei-Fei, L.: ImageNet: a large-scale hierarchical image database. In: 2009 IEEE Conference on Computer Vision and Pattern Recognition, pp. 248–255. IEEE (2009)
13. Esteva, A., et al.: Dermatologist-level classification of skin cancer with deep neural networks. Nature **542**(7639), 115–118 (2017)
14. He, K., Zhang, X., Ren, S., Sun, J.: Deep residual learning for image recognition. In: Proceedings of the IEEE Conference on Computer Vision and Pattern Recognition, pp. 770–778 (2016)
15. Huang, G., Liu, Z., Van Der Maaten, L., Weinberger, K.Q.: Densely connected convolutional networks. In: Proceedings of the IEEE Conference on Computer Vision and Pattern Recognition, pp. 4700–4708 (2017)
16. ISIC: Skin lesion analysis towards melanoma detection. International skin imaging collaboration (2019). https://www.isic-archive.com. Accessed 26 Feb 2022
17. Jetley, S., Lord, N.A., Lee, N., Torr, P.H.: Learn to pay attention. In: International Conference on Learning Representations (2018)
18. Kharazmi, P., Kalia, S., Lui, H., Wang, Z., Lee, T.: A feature fusion system for basal cell carcinoma detection through data-driven feature learning and patient profile. Skin Res. Technol. **24**(2), 256–264 (2018)
19. Li, W., Zhuang, J., Wang, R., Zhang, J., Zheng, W.S.: Fusing metadata and dermoscopy images for skin disease diagnosis. In: 2020 IEEE 17th International Symposium on Biomedical Imaging (ISBI), pp. 1996–2000. IEEE (2020)
20. Lin, T.Y., RoyChowdhury, A., Maji, S.: Bilinear CNN models for fine-grained visual recognition. In: Proceedings of the IEEE International Conference on Computer Vision, pp. 1449–1457 (2015)

21. Liu, Y., Chen, X., Cheng, J., Peng, H.: A medical image fusion method based on convolutional neural networks. In: 2017 20th International Conference on Information Fusion (Fusion), pp. 1–7. IEEE (2017)
22. Pacheco, A.G., Krohling, R.A.: Recent advances in deep learning applied to skin cancer detection. arXiv preprint arXiv:1912.03280 (2019)
23. Pacheco, A.G., Krohling, R.A.: The impact of patient clinical information on automated skin cancer detection. Comput. Biol. Med. **116**, 103545 (2020)
24. Pacheco, A.G.C., Krohling, R.: An attention-based mechanism to combine images and metadata in deep learning models applied to skin cancer classification. IEEE J. Biomed. Health Inform. **25**, 3554–3563 (2021)
25. Pedregosa, F., et al.: Scikit-learn: machine learning in Python. J. Mach. Learn. Res. **12**, 2825–2830 (2011)
26. Sandler, M., Howard, A., Zhu, M., Zhmoginov, A., Chen, L.C.: MobileNetV 2: inverted residuals and linear bottlenecks. In: Proceedings of the IEEE Conference on Computer Vision and Pattern Recognition, pp. 4510–4520 (2018)
27. Simonyan, K., Zisserman, A.: Very deep convolutional networks for large-scale image recognition. arXiv preprint arXiv:1409.1556 (2014)
28. Tan, M., Le, Q.: EfficientNet: rethinking model scaling for convolutional neural networks. In: International Conference on Machine Learning, pp. 6105–6114. PMLR (2019)
29. Tschandl, P., Rosendahl, C., Kittler, H.: The HAM10000 dataset, a large collection of multi-source dermatoscopic images of common pigmented skin lesions. Sci. Data **5**(1), 1–9 (2018)
30. WHO: Ultraviolet (UV) radiation and skin cancer (2022). https://www.who.int/news-room/questions-and-answers/item/radiation-ultraviolet-(uv)-radiation-and-skin-cancer. Accessed on 26.02.2022
31. Yu, Z., Jiang, X., Zhou, F., Qin, J., Ni, D., Chen, S., Lei, B., Wang, T.: Melanoma recognition in dermoscopy images via aggregated deep convolutional features. IEEE Trans. Biomed. Eng. **66**(4), 1006–1016 (2018)

Predicting Osteoarthritis of the Temporomandibular Joint Using Random Forest with Privileged Information

Elisa Warner[1], Najla Al-Turkestani[1,2], Jonas Bianchi[3],
Marcela Lima Gurgel[1], Lucia Cevidanes[1(✉)], and Arvind Rao[1(✉)]

[1] University of Michigan, Ann Arbor, MI 48109, USA
{elisawa,alnajla,mlimagur,luciacev,ukarvind}@umich.edu
[2] King Abdulaziz University, Jeddah 22254, Saudi Arabia
[3] University of the Pacific, San Francisco, CA 94103, USA
jbianchi@pacific.edu

Abstract. Osteoarthritis of the temporomandibular joint (TMJ OA) is the most common disorder of the TMJ. A clinical decision support (CDS) system designed to detect TMJ OA could function as a useful screening tool as part of regular check-ups to detect early onset. This study implements a CDS concept model based on Random Forest and dubbed RF$^+$ to predict TMJ OA with the hypothesis that a model which leverages high-resolution radiological and biomarker data in training only can improve predictions compared with a baseline model which does not use privileged information. We found that the RF$^+$ model can outperform the baseline model even when privileged features are not of gold standard quality. Additionally, we introduce a novel method for post-hoc feature analysis, finding shortRunHighGreyLevelEmphasis of the lateral condyles and joint distance to be the most important features from the privileged modalities for predicting TMJ OA.

Keywords: Temporomandibular joint · Privileged learning · Multimodal learning

1 Introduction

The temporomandibular joint (TMJ) plays an essential role in mouth movement and consists of a complex system of bone, cartilage and muscle. Osteoarthritis of the TMJ (TMJ OA), a degenerative disease which affects all structures therein, is the most common disorder of the TMJ [13]. Observations from radiological images show TMJ OA is associated with flattening or deformation of the lateral

Supplementary Information The online version contains supplementary material available at https://doi.org/10.1007/978-3-031-23223-7_7.

J. S. H. Baxter et al. (Eds.): EPIMI 2022/ML-CDS 2022/TDA4BiomedicalImaging 2022,
LNCS 13755, pp. 77–86, 2022.
https://doi.org/10.1007/978-3-031-23223-7_7

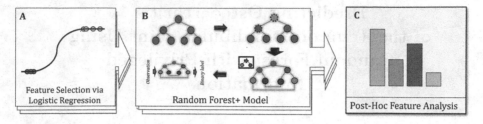

Fig. 1. Workflow for the reported study. In this study, we utilize Leave-One-Out Cross Validation on a sample of 97 patients. For each fold, a feature selection process consisting of Logistic Regression is computed (A), and then a Random Forest$^+$ model is constructed based on the selected features (B). After all folds have been calculated, a post-hoc analysis is conducted to determine the most important privileged and non-privileged features for tree-based transforms.

condyles, reduction of joint space, and possible alterations to the articular fossa region [8,12]. Although prevalence of TMJ OA has been difficult to calculate, post-mortem analysis of modern bone collections have found a 30.2% prevalence among modern humans [8], with 40 to 75% of the population reporting at least one symptom of overall disorders of the TMJ (TMD) [12]. TMJ OA falls under the umbrella of osteoarthritis, which is the second most prevalent musculoskeletal disorder behind lower back pain, occurring with a global incidence of nearly 15,000 per year [16] (Fig. 1).

Recently, clinical decision support (CDS) models have made waves in the medical community, assisting in diagnosis of a wide range of conditions [1,9,14]. Although CDS models cannot replace the need for experienced dental experts, a CDS system designed to detect TMJ OA could function as a useful screening tool as part of regular check-ups, with the goal of detecting early TMJ OA and thus permitting dental experts to initiate treatment and preventive behavioral strategies to decelerate degradation of the TMJ at an early stage.

While clinical questionnaires designed to screen for TMD may help screen for TMJ OA, we hypothesize that including radiological imaging information from the TMJ site as well as protein biomarkers collected from serum/saliva could provide additional information which may be useful for discriminating TMJ OA patients from healthy patients. Studies analyzing protein biomarkers and radiological information in TMJ OA patients have already asserted the predictive utility of these features [3,17].

However, although radiological imaging and protein biomarkers could be useful additions to a TMJ OA CDS model, it is not reasonable to expect that most clinics would be able to provide such data, as high-resolution cone-beam computed tomography (CBCT) scans of the articular fossa and lateral condyle regions of the TMJ as well as protein microarrays of human serum and saliva samples are more common in research rather than clinical practice. Since typical predictive models require all modalities to be present with no missing data, multimodal co-learning strategies must be explored.

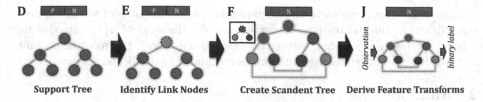

Fig. 2. Workflow of the RF^+ framework using tree-based feature transforms. The top bar of the figure indicates the feature space used (N or ($N \bigcup P$)).

One such strategy incorporating privileged information was developed as a part of a concept called "knowledge transfer" [15]. In knowledge transfer models, a "privileged" modality of data exists in the model solely as a "teacher", providing information which assists the "student" model solely during the training phase, while disappearing in the test phase. With proper knowledge transfer, the final student model should perform more accurately with the assistance of the privileged information during training than without. In this study, we consider multimodal models which incorporate privileged information, where clinical features will be considered non-privileged information available in training and testing and radiological and biomarker features will be considered privileged information available in the training set only. This will allow the latter, rarer modalities to still assist the model while only requiring basic clinical questionnaire information at test-time, thus generalizing such a decision support model to a larger audience.

The most common privileged learning frameworks are based on artificial neural network (ANN) or support vector machine (SVM) frameworks [5,6,15,17]. However, these models work best under very specific conditions. ANNs are primarily useful with large data samples and features, but considered largely inappropriate for smaller datasets due to the scale of trained parameters required. The well-known SVM^+ model, a framework of SVM designed specifically to incorporate privileged information, can be problematic because the privileged modality functions as an error corrector in the model. This means that the privileged modality must provide discriminatory capabilities equivalent to a gold standard, or risk introduction of erroneous error corrections, thus reducing AUCs of the student model. Although some models such as [10] have attempted modifications of the SVM^+ algorithm to improve upon this shortcoming, such models are not widely available and come with large computational overhead. In another model, [7] developed a Random Forest model which incorporates privileged information through the construction of "tree-based feature transforms". The authors claimed that their model can perform at least as well as a non-privileged model, even in the case of substandard privileged information, because of the Random Forest's unique ability to select best features from a given feature bag.

This study implements a CDS concept model based on the framework from [7] for predicting TMJ OA vs healthy controls, with the hypothesis that a model which leverages our available high-resolution radiological and biomarker data in training can improve predictions compared with a baseline model which requires only clinical features in testing. We further expand the work of [7] by introducing a novel method for post-hoc feature analysis, tracing back the most important features for prediction among both privileged and non-privileged feature sets.

2   Methods

2.1   Data Acquisition and Preparation

Our dataset consisted of 51 early-stage TMJ OA patients and 50 healthy controls recruited at the University of Michigan. All the diagnoses were confirmed by a TMD and orofacial pain specialist following the Diagnostic Criteria for Temporo-mandibular Disorders (DC/TMD) [11]. The clinical, biological and radiographic data described below were collected from TMJ OA and control subjects with informed consent and following the guidelines of the Institutional Review Board HUM00113199.

Details on the dataset can be found in [3]. Briefly, the clinical dataset was collected following DC/TMD criteria. The biological data comprised of proteins that were previously correlated with arthritis initiation, progression and bone morphological alterations [4]. Using customized protein microarrays (Ray-Biotech, Inc. Norcross, GA), the expression level of 13 proteins was measured in the participants' saliva and serum samples, respectively. The radiological data was collected from CBCT scans taken using 3D Accuitomo machine (J. Morita MFG. CORP Tokyo, Japan). It consisted of 3D superior condylar-to-fossa joint space measurements and radiomic features. Using BoneTexture module from 3D-Slicer software (www.3Dslicer.org), 43 radiomic features were attained following a standardized protocol reported by Bianchi et al. [2].

Of the 101 patients obtained, four were removed due to missing data, resulting in a final sample size of 97 patients. Features were split into "privileged" and "non-privileged" information based on their probable availability in a real-world clinical setting. Due to the greater difficulty of obtaining high-resolution CBCT scans and microarray biological samples in a clinical setting, we classified these modalities as privileged information while the clinical data were marked as non-privileged features. In total, 68 privileged features and six non-privileged features were included in the dataset.

2.2   Model Construction

The primary model utilized in this study, which here is dubbed "RF$^+$", is based on the tree-based feature transforms framework from [7] and illustrated in Figure Fig 2. In our RF$^+$ model, a Random Forest model called the "support forest" consisting of K decision trees is first constructed based on both privileged features ($\{P\}$) and non-privileged features ($\{N\}$) in the training set only (Fig 2D). After the support forest is constructed, a simple algorithm searches through all nodes of each tree $t_k, k = 1 \ldots K$ to identify nodes of interest called "link nodes" (Fig 2E). In order to qualify as a link node, any node n_i^k from tree k must satisfy at one of the following criteria:

1. Node n_i^k is a root node
2. Node n_i^k has a parent n_{i-1}^k with a node feature $f_{i-1}^k \in N$ and n_i^k has a node feature $f_i^k \in P$
3. Node n_i^k has a parent n_{i-1}^k with a node feature $f_{i-1}^k \in P$ and n_i^k has a node feature $f_i^k \in N$.

For each link node, the observations at the left and right children of the node are annotated as "0" and "1", respectively. Then, these labels are utilized to train a "scandent tree" for each link node, which attempts to replicate the discriminative power of the link node utilizing only non-privileged features (Fig 2F).

After all scandent trees are formulated, "tree-based feature transforms" are constructed for each data observation based on the label assigned by each scandent tree. Therefore, if z link nodes are discovered, then z scandent trees are formulated, resulting in z number of binary-labeled tree-based feature transforms (Fig 2J). Then, a final model is formulated based on the non-privileged features and tree-based features only. Since the scandent trees are also based only on non-privileged features, no privileged features are required in testing.

2.3 Cross Validation and Evaluation

Two types of cross validation were utilized in this study. The first was Leave-One-Out Cross Validation (LOOCV), due to its ability to demonstrate fullest use of the training data in a single run. In order to provide a more robust study, we also incorporated a second validation method consisting of 400 times random bootstrapping of 15% of the dataset. Because this method is essentially "Out-of-Bag" sampling for Random Forest models, we denote this validation method with the acronym "OOB" from here onward.

For comparative analysis, four additional models were constructed: 1) one consisting of only privileged features, 2) one consisting of both non-privileged and privileged features, 3) one with only tree-based features, 4) the Baseline model, consisting of only non-privileged features. All models were evaluated for Area Under the Receiver Operating Curve (AUC) for both LOO and OOB validation methods, and standard error was calculated. For OOB, mean AUC and mean standard error were calculated, respectively.

2.4 Post-hoc Feature Analysis

Finally, after all models were run, a post-hoc feature analysis was performed on the tree-based feature transforms. For each tree-based feature transform, we traced back the link node from which it was based and analyzed the node feature at that link node. We then totaled up the frequency with which each feature appeared as a node feature for a link node. Based on the definition of a link node, we decided to distinguish a feature at a link node as a "Root" feature if the node feature appeared at a link node defined by criteria 1 for identifying link nodes (See Sect. 2.2). This is because criteria 2 and 3 for defining link nodes are based on node features of a node given the node feature of a parent node. Thus, although our feature analysis identifies a specific feature at a link node, for non-"Root" features, the scandent tree formed for the link node listed will try to replicate the discriminatory ability of the node feature at the link node given settings of previous node features. Scandent trees from "Root" features, by contrast, will try to replicate the discriminatory ability of the node feature only.

2.5   Implementation

Due to the large number of privileged features, some of which may not be important, a univariate logistic regression to predict TMJ OA was run on the training set for each fold *before* initiating the RF^+ model workflow. Namely, only privileged features were analyzed by logistic regression, and privileged features with an AUC > 0.55 were included in the RF^+ model. Because there were only six variables included in the non-privileged feature set, all non-privileged variables were included for all folds.

The model implementation from [7] was preserved in our work. Namely, a feature bagging size of $\sqrt{num}$ of features was implemented, and the entire training set was utilized in the construction of the scandent trees. In order to reduce the number of unimportant tree-based features, we implemented a feature importance calculation on the training set immediately after construction of the features and features with an importance score of 0 were eliminated. Due to the large imbalance of non-privileged and tree-based feature transforms, we force equal sampling of each feature set to construct each tree in the final forest. We set max depth equal to 7 and number of trees equal to 100.

3   Results and Discussion

3.1   Dataset Analysis

A patient demographic data table with sample sizes and summaries of the baseline data can be shown in Table S1. As expected, clinical questions for TMD demonstrated discriminative ability to discern TMJ OA from healthy control patients. Averages for privileged information were omitted to save space.

3.2   Feature Selection Analysis

Results from the feature selection using univariate Logistic Regression are shown in Table S2 ranked by the percent of folds in which the features were included as well as the average AUC across all 97 folds. Included in the table was also the performance of non-privileged variables.

Table 1. Model comparison results

Model	LOO AUC	LOO stderr	OOB AUC	OOB stderr
Privileged only	0.6390	0.0252	0.6163	0.0513
Baseline+Privileged	0.7198	0.0267	0.7184	0.0530
RF$^+$	**0.6798**	**0.0306**	**0.6974**	0.0602
Tree-based only	0.6692	0.0477	0.6535	0.0939
Baseline	0.6518	0.0309	0.6940	**0.0590**

3.3 Model Results

AUCs and their respective standard errors for each tested model are shown in Table 1 and Fig S1. The top box (top two models) consists of models in which privileged features are included in the test set, while the bottom box (bottom three models) consists of models in which only non-privileged features are included in the test set. The proposed RF$^+$ model outperformed both the Baseline model as well as the model based on tree-based feature transforms alone. Interestingly, while the Baseline+Privileged model (which incorporates privileged features during testing) outperforms all other models as expected, the Privileged Only model performs lower than expected, even when a Logistic Regression is used for feature selection. This may indicate that although radiomic images are useful for detecting TMJ OA, the extracted features themselves may not be a better screen of TMJ OA compared to a simple clinical questionnaire, but when combined with the clinical questions, can provide some supplementary information.

The improved performance of the Tree-Based Only model over the Baseline model demonstrates the potential for tree-based feature transforms to mimic the predictive power of privileged features with only non-privileged features, and suggests that with only six non-privileged features, this model can still coax out interesting non-linear relationships between existing features that were not easily ascertained otherwise.

Lastly, the performance of the RF$^+$ model is interesting in that it can improve the baseline model, even where privileged features are not a "gold standard" source of information, confirming the advantages of this model stated in [7]. In privileged learning models where privileged information is utilized as an "error corrector" [15], privileged features must be close to gold standard quality in order to prevent introduction of erroneous error corrections to a non-privileged model. However, with tree-based transforms, when privileged information is poor, a decision tree can choose tree-based transforms which originate from a non-privileged root node if it outperforms those originating from privileged root nodes. Thus, the RF$^+$ can leverage the discriminative capabilities of privileged features, while downplaying weaknesses of the features.

3.4 Feature Importance Based on Tree-Based Feature Transforms

Feature importance for the top 20 features is shown in Fig. 3. Frequencies were rescaled into a score in range $[0, 1]$ by dividing all feature frequencies by the

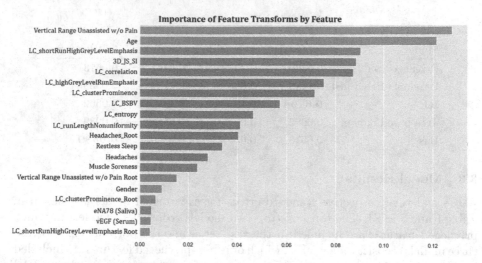

Fig. 3. Top 20 features derived from tree-based feature transforms and their respective importance scores.

total number of feature appearances. The top features were Vertical Range Unassisted w/o Pain, which is a clinical feature whereby a patient is asked to open their mouth to the fullest range before pain is felt. The most important privileged features were shortRunHighGreyLevelEmphasis of the lateral condyle and 3D_JS_SI (joint distances). Of the top 10 unique privileged features which ranked highest using this method, eight also appeared in the top 10 most predictive privileged features from the Logistic Regression rankings in Table S2.

4 Conclusion

In this study we implemented an RF$^+$ CDS concept model based on tree-based feature transforms to detect TMJ OA in 97 patients. We incorporate two modalities of privileged information, namely radiological imaging features and biomarker protein data, and one set of non-privileged information consisting of clinical questionnaire data. We demonstrated that our proposed RF$^+$ model outperforms the baseline model, even though both models use only non-privileged information at test time. Furthermore, we expand upon the RF$^+$ model framework to incorporate our own feature importance scores based on appearance of link node features among the most popular tree-based features in the RF$^+$ framework. We show that tree-based feature transforms identify some of the most discriminative features of the dataset and sufficiently replicate their discriminatory capabilities with non-privileged clinical features alone. This work demonstrates both the usefulness of RF$^+$ in predicting TMJ OA and elucidates benefits of incorporating research-obtained information that is not normally obtained clinically as a means to improve upon CDS models.

Acknowledgements. E.W. and A.R. are supported by NIH Grant R37-CA214955. E.W. was supported by T32GM070449 as well. This study was supported by NIDCR R01DE024450 and AAOF Graber Family Teaching and Research Award and by Research Enhancement Award Activity 141 from the University of the Pacific, School of Dentistry.

References

1. Ackermann, K., Baker, J., Green, M., et al.: Computerized clinical decision support systems for the early detection of sepsis among adult inpatients: scoping review. J. Med. Internet Res. **24**(2), e31083 (2022). https://doi.org/10.2196/31083
2. Bianchi, J., Gonçalves, J.R., de Oliveira Ruellas, A.C., et al.: Software comparison to analyze bone radiomics from high resolution CBCT scans of mandibular condyles. Dentomaxillofacial Radiol. **48**(6), 20190049 (2019). https://doi.org/10.1259/dmfr.20190049
3. Bianchi, J., de Oliveira Ruellas, A.C., Gonçalves, J.R., et al.: Osteoarthritis of the temporomandibular joint can be diagnosed earlier using biomarkers and machine learning. Sci. Rep. **10**(1) (2020). https://doi.org/10.1038/s41598-020-64942-0
4. Cevidanes, L., Walker, D., Schilling, J., et al.: 3d osteoarthritic changes in TMJ condylar morphology correlates with specific systemic and local biomarkers of disease. Osteoarthritis Cartilage **22**(10), 1657–1667 (2014). https://doi.org/10.1016/j.joca.2014.06.014
5. Chauhan, G., Liao, R., Wells, W., et al.: Joint modeling of chest radiographs and radiology reports for pulmonary EDEMA assessment (2020). https://doi.org/10.48550/ARXIV.2008.09884, https://arxiv.org/abs/2008.09884
6. Hu, M., et al.: Knowledge distillation from multi-modal to mono-modal segmentation networks. In: Martel, A.L., et al. (eds.) MICCAI 2020. LNCS, vol. 12261, pp. 772–781. Springer, Cham (2020). https://doi.org/10.1007/978-3-030-59710-8_75
7. Moradi, M., Syeda-Mahmood, T., Hor, S.: Tree-based transforms for privileged learning. In: Wang, L., Adeli, E., Wang, Q., Shi, Y., Suk, H.-I. (eds.) MLMI 2016. LNCS, vol. 10019, pp. 188–195. Springer, Cham (2016). https://doi.org/10.1007/978-3-319-47157-0_23
8. Rando, C., Waldron, T.: TMJ osteoarthritis: a new approach to diagnosis. Am. J. Phys. Anthropol. **148**(1), 45–53 (2012). https://doi.org/10.1002/ajpa.22039
9. Rao, A., Palma, J.: Clinical decision support in the neonatal ICU. Seminars Fetal Neonatal Med. 101332 (2022). https://doi.org/10.1016/j.siny.2022.101332
10. Sabeti, E., Drews, J., Reamaroon, N., et al.: Learning using partially available privileged information and label uncertainty: application in detection of acute respiratory distress syndrome. IEEE J. Biomed. Health Inform. **25**(3), 784–796 (2021). https://doi.org/10.1109/jbhi.2020.3008601
11. Schiffman, E., Ohrbach, R., Truelove, E., et al.: Diagnostic criteria for temporomandibular disorders (DC/TMD) for clinical and research applications: recommendations of the international RDC/TMD consortium network and orofacial pain special interest group. J. Oral Facial Pain Headache **28**(1), 6–27 (2014). https://doi.org/10.11607/jop.1151
12. Scrivani, S.J., Keith, D.A., Kaban, L.B.: Temporomandibular disorders. New Engl. J. Med. **359**(25), 2693–2705 (2008). https://doi.org/10.1056/nejmra0802472
13. Tanaka, E., Detamore, M., Mercuri, L.: Degenerative disorders of the temporomandibular joint: etiology, diagnosis, and treatment. J. Dental Res. **87**(4), 296–307 (2008). https://doi.org/10.1177/154405910808700406

14. Tuppad, A., Patil, S.D.: Machine learning for diabetes clinical decision support: a review. Adv. Comput. Intell. **2**(2), 1–24 (2022). https://doi.org/10.1007/s43674-022-00034-y
15. Vapnik, V., Vashist, A.: A new learning paradigm: learning using privileged information. Neural Netw. **22**(5–6), 544–557 (2009). https://doi.org/10.1016/j.neunet.2009.06.042
16. Vos, T., Abajobir, A.A., Abate, K.H., et al.: Global, regional, and national incidence, prevalence, and years lived with disability for 328 diseases and injuries for 195 countries, 1990–2016: a systematic analysis for the global burden of disease study 2016. Lancet **390**(10100), 1211–1259 (2017). https://doi.org/10.1016/s0140-6736(17)32154-2
17. Zhang, W., Bianchi, J., Turkestani, N.A., et al.: Temporomandibular joint osteoarthritis diagnosis using privileged learning of protein markers. In: 2021 43rd Annual International Conference of the IEEE Engineering in Medicine & Biology Society (EMBC). IEEE (2021). https://doi.org/10.1109/embc46164.2021.9629990

Hybrid Network Based on Cross-Modal Feature Fusion for Diagnosis of Alzheimer's Disease

Zifeng Qiu, Peng Yang, Tianfu Wang, and Baiying Lei(✉)

National-Regional Key Technology Engineering Laboratory for Medical Ultrasound, Guangdong Key Laboratory for Biomedical Measurements and Ultrasound Imaging, School of Biomedical Engineering, Health Science Center, Shenzhen University, Shenzhen, China
leiby@szu.edu.cn

Abstract. Early diagnosis of Alzheimer's disease (AD) (e.g., mild cognitive impairment, MCI), timely intervention, and treatment will effectively delay the further development of AD. Structural Magnetic Resonance Imaging (sMRI) and Positron Emission Computed Tomography (PET) play an essential role in diagnosing AD and MCI as they show signs of morphological changes in brain atrophy. However, it is difficult to learn more comprehensive information to diagnose AD and MCI thoroughly by single-modality brain imaging data, and it is challenging to locate the lesion area accurately. For diagnosing AD and MCI, convolutional neural networks (CNNs) have shown quite promising performance. However, the ability of CNNs to model global information is limited due to the properties of CNN sliding windows. In contrast, Transformer lacks modeling of local invariance, but it utilizes a self-attention mechanism to model long-term dependencies. Therefore, a novel cross-modal feature fusion based CNN-Transformer framework for AD and MCI diagnosis has been proposed. Specifically, we firstly exploit a large kernel attention (LKA) module to learn the attention map. Then, there will be two branches, CNN and Transformer, which are utilized to extract higher-level local and global features further. Furthermore, we utilize a modality feature fusion block to fuse the features of the two modalities. The extensive experimental results on the ADNI dataset show that our model outperforms the state-of-the-art methods.

Keywords: Alzheimer's disease diagnosis · Structural magnetic resonance imaging · Positron emission computed tomography · Large kernel attention

1 Introduction

Alzheimer's disease (AD) is an irreversible progressive neurodegenerative disease. It is reported that there are currently estimated to be over 55 million people worldwide living with dementia, which is expected to skyrocket to 139 million by 2050 [1]. Mild cognitive impairment (MCI) is an early stage of AD, and it can be subdivided into pMCI and sMCI according to whether it converts to AD. Diagnosing patients at the time of MCI facilitate intervention and treatment to delay progression to AD. Since structural

© The Author(s), under exclusive license to Springer Nature Switzerland AG 2022
J. S. H. Baxter et al. (Eds.): EPIMI 2022/ML-CDS 2022/TDA4BiomedicalImaging 2022,
LNCS 13755, pp. 87–99, 2022.
https://doi.org/10.1007/978-3-031-23223-7_8

magnetic resonance imaging (sMRI) can provide an intuitive way of observing brain structure changes, many studies to diagnose AD have been developed through sMRI-based analysis [2–4]. In addition, positron emission computed tomography (PET) is also widely used in diagnosing AD due to its high sensitivity and specificity [5, 6]. Different from unimodal brain imaging, using bimodal or even multimodal brain imaging can extract more useful information to assist the diagnosis of AD. Therefore, more and more studies are beginning to use multimodal data such as sMRI data and PET data for AD diagnosis [5, 7, 8].

Generally, traditional machine learning methods require complex preprocessing to obtain hand-crafted classification features [9]. As a common and typical deep learning method, convolutional neural network (CNN) can extract the most discriminative features hierarchically, which shows excellent performance in end-to-end AD diagnosis. However, traditional CNN focuses on local features and ignores the global information of images. Since the Depthwise Separable Convolution (DSC) [10] has fewer parameters and computation than the usual convolution and can improve the performance of the model, many networks have used it to achieved good performance using [11–13]. Since Transformer can effectively extract the characteristics of global information, some scholars have studied the use of Transformer to diagnose AD. However, Vision Transformer [14] usually requires a large amount of additional data and longer training time to achieve better performance, which causes difficulties in practical image task applications. One reason for this phenomenon is that the self-attention mechanism treats 2D images as 1D sequence, which destroys the key 2D structure of the images and ignores the modeling of inductive biases specific to vision tasks.

To detect AD accurately, we propose a novel hybrid framework based on cross-modal feature fusion. Different from the previous methods, we first leverage a large kernel attention (LKA) module to generate attention maps with discriminative information. Then, we send the attention map to the CNN branch and the Transformer branch, respectively, and the two branches will perform a feature fusion at each stage to learn more comprehensive information. Our main contributions are as follows:

- A novel end-to-end hybrid framework is proposed. We leverage a large convolutional kernel and consider the inductive bias to learn feature representations.
- A feature fusion block is designed. We fully consider the similarity and specificity between different features.
- A framework for early AD diagnosis based on multimodal data is designed. We make full use of structural and functional features to improve diagnostic accuracy.

2 Methodology

2.1 Method Overview

Figure 1 is the framework of our model, which consists of three parts, attention weight learning, feature extraction, and classification decision. Compared with the use of complete 3D images for training, we chose to train with one slice as the main and the other two as supplements, in order to reduce the computational overhead and improve the efficiency of the model. To improve the accuracy of the learned features, we first use an attention module consisting of large kernel convolutions to generate attention maps to assist the high-level feature learning of the backbone network. Next, the learned network is sent to the feature extraction backbone. The backbone network of our model consists of four stages. Each stage consists of two branches, the CNN branch consisting of ResNet50 and multi-head attention and the Transformer branch consisting of reduction cell and normal cells.

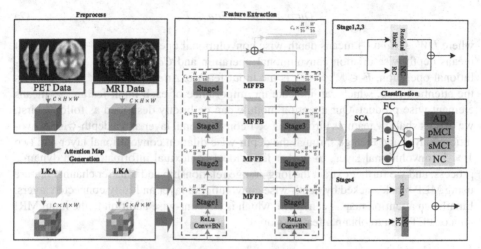

Fig. 1. Illustration of the proposed method. Our proposed method consists of four parts, preprocess, attention weight learning, feature extraction, and classification decision.

The unique ability of CNN to learn local information and the global modeling ability of Transformer combine to learn feature representations better. Meanwhile, to take full advantage of the similarity and specificity between the two modal information, we design a modal feature fusion block to strengthen the interconnection between modalities and improve the comprehensiveness of the learned features. After learning the high-level features, we further use the spatial information-channel attention to learn the spatial and channel information of the high-level features. Finally, we use the Softmax classifier for classification.

3 Large Kernel Attention Module

The attention mechanism can identify the discriminative features and automatically ignore noisy responses according to the inputs features. Then, attention mechanism produces an attention map, which plays an essential role in image classification.

The most well-known attention mechanism to build the relationship between different parts is self-attention (SA). However, SA has obvious shortcomings when it is applied in computer vision, such as it only achieves spatial adaptability but ignores the channel adaptability. Another way to produce an attention map is to use the large kernel convolution [15, 16], while large kernel convolution brings substantial computational overhead. Therefore, combining the attention mechanism and large kernel convolution seems to be a better way to produce an attention map. Specifically, large kernel convolutional operations can be divided into three components. As shown at the top of Fig. 2, the LKA can be written as:

$$Attention = Conv_{1 \times 1}(DW - D - Conv_{1 \times 1}(DW - Conv(F))), \quad (1)$$

$$Output = Attention \otimes F, \quad (2)$$

where $DW - Conv(\cdot)$ means depth-wise convolutional operation, $DW - D - Conv(\cdot)$ means depth-wise dilation convolutional operation and $Conv(\cdot)$ means 1×1 convolutional operation, $F \in \mathbb{R}^{C \times H \times W}$ is the input feature. $Attention \in \mathbb{R}^{C \times H \times W}$ denotes the attention map, which can indicate the importance of each input feature. $\otimes$ means element-wise product. Our attention module can be briefly described as follows: first, we extract shallow features through a 1×1 convolutional layer and a depth-wise convolutional layer and then go through the depth-wise dilation convolutional layer and two 1×1 convolutional layers to further learn local contextual information and dynamic process, and we further extract the long--range relationship and transfer channel feature using MLP block stacked by depth-wise convolutional layer and fully connected layers. Finally, an attention map is generated, which is element-wise addition to the input MRI data or PET data to obtain a feature map.

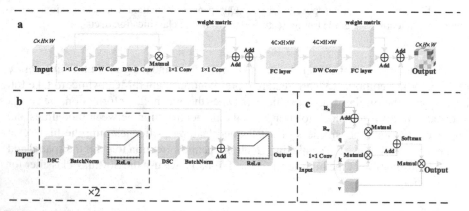

Fig. 2. **a.** Illustration of LKA module. LKA combines the advantages of convolution and self-attention. It considers the local contextual information, large receptive field, and dynamic process. **b.** Illustration of the residual block. We use depth-wise separable convolution to replace normal convolutional operation. **c.** Illustration of Multi-Head Self-Attention.

3.1 CNN Branch

In recent years, CNNs are universally performed on the 2D slices of brain MRI and PET for AD diagnosis. CNNs focus on the learning and extraction of local information, while global information is crucial for MRI and PET brain images. SA mechanism can capture global information, which plays an important role in AD diagnosis research of MRI data and PET data. Therefore, incorporating attention mechanism into CNN can better improve the performance.

Different from previous CNNs, we design a shallow neural network due to the limited subjects of the dataset. We use depthwise separable convolution(DSC) to replace the convolutional design of our CNN branch. We use the convolutional layer and residual module to design our CNN model. There are only one convolutional layer and three residual blocks. The residual module is shown in Fig. 2b. To catch the global information of the brain images, we add Multi-Head Self-Attention (MHSA) behind the residual module. The MHSA is shown in Fig. 2c.

In the first three stage, Our CNN branch can be expressed as:

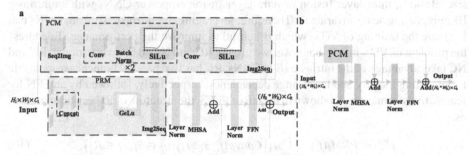

Fig. 3. Illustration of reduction cell (RC) and normal cell (NC). RC and NC share a simple basic structure, while RC has an extra pyramid reduction module using atrous convolutions with different dilation rates to embed multi-scale context into tokens.

$$f_{h1} = ReLu(BN(DSC(f_i))), \tag{3}$$

$$f_{h2} = ReLu(BN(DSC(f_{h1}))), \tag{4}$$

$$Output = ReLu(BN(DSC(f_{h2}) + f_i)), \tag{5}$$

In the last stage, our CNN branch can be expressed as:

$$q, k, v = Conv_{1 \times 1}(f_i), \tag{6}$$

$$Content = q \otimes k, \tag{7}$$

$$Position = q \otimes (R_h + R_w), \tag{8}$$

$$Output = v \otimes Softmax(Content + Position), \tag{9}$$

where $f_i \in \mathbb{R}^{C \times H \times W}$ is the input feature, q, k, v represent query key and value, respectively, $R_h \in \mathbb{R}^{C \times H \times W}$ and $R_w \in \mathbb{R}^{C \times H \times W}$ are relative position encodings consistent with the input feature dimension.

3.2 Transformer Branch

Vision Transformer (ViT) is an extended application of Transformer in the field of computer vision, and has achieved great success in various vision tasks. Specifically, ViT splits the images to several small patches, and each patch is recorded as a token. After rearranging all tokens into a sequence, it is directly input into the Transformer network to extract feature. But ViT requires large-scale training data and a longer training schedule, which causes difficulty applying to MRI or PET. One important reason is that ViT lacks specific inductive bias (IB) in modeling vision tasks, such as modeling local correlations and scale invariance of brain images, which leads to the inability of model to utilize MRI or PET data efficiently and affects the model performance. CNNs have the intrinsic IB in the model locality due to the convolutional operation in CNNs extracting local features from the neighbor pixels within the receptive field determined by the kernel size. Besides, inter-layer fusion or intra-layer fusion empower CNNs with an intrinsic IB in modeling scale-invariance. Therefore, leveraging the intrinsic IB from CNNs can facilitate the training of ViTs, which is helpful to improve the performance. To address the problem of ViTs in AD diagnosis, we use the RC and NC to build our model. RC and NC take advantage of the intrinsic IB in CNNs. RC has two parallel branches responsible for modeling locality and long-range dependency, respectively, followed by an FFN for feature transformation. As shown in the left of Fig. 3, the structure of RC can be expressed as:

$$f_i^{ms} \triangleq PRM_i(f_i) = Cat\left(\left[Conv_{ij}\left(f_i; s_{ij}; r_i\right)|s_{ij} \in S_i, r_i \in R\right]\right), \tag{10}$$

$$f_i^g = MHSA_i\left(Img2Seq\left(f_i^{ms}\right)\right), \tag{11}$$

$$f_i^{lg} = f_i^g + PCM_i(f_i), \tag{12}$$

$$f_{i+1} = Seq2Img\left(FFN_i\left(f_i^{lg}\right) + f_i^{lg}\right), \tag{13}$$

where $f_i \in \mathbb{R}^{H_1 \times W_1 \times C_1}$ denote the input feature of the i_{th} RC, $Conv(\cdot)$ is the j-th convolutional layer in the pyramid reduction module (PRM), $Img2Seq(\cdot)$ is a reshape operation to flatten the feature map to a 1D sequence, $PCM_i(\cdot)$ is a parallel convolutional module (PCM), which is composed of three stacked convolutional layers and an $Img2Seq(\cdot)$ operation, $Seq2Img(\cdot)$ is the reverse operation of $Img2Seq(\cdot)$, a reshape operation reshapes the sequence back to feature maps. NC is similar to RC without PRM, as shown in the right of Fig. 3. It is unnecessary to use PRM in NC due to the feature maps after processing by RC have already gotten relatively small spatial size.

3.3 Modal Feature Fusion Block

Single-modality brain images can extract less information, while multimodal data can be used to learn more information to effectively assist AD diagnosis. Therefore, in order to take full advantage of the complementary relationship and specificity of the two modalities of MRI and PET, we design a modal feature fusion module (MFFB), which

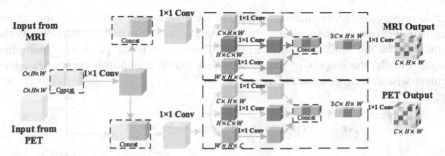

Fig. 4. Illustration of the modal feature fusion module which receives the MRI and PET features obtained from each stage as input and outputs the learned MRI and PET features via the obtained similarity and specificity of the two modalities. It first learns the similarity of MRI feature and PET feature, then use dimensional convolution to learn the specificity of the two modalities.

receives the MRI and PET features obtained from each stage as input, and outputs the learned features obtained from the similarity and specificity of the two modalities, the specific flow of MFFB is shown in Fig. 4. Specifically, after inputting the two modal features $X_{MRI} \in \mathbb{R}^{C \times H \times W}$ and $X_{PET} \in \mathbb{R}^{C \times H \times W}$, the features of the two modalities are spliced together, through a layer of 1×1 convolutional layer to learn their similarity features $f_{fusion} \in \mathbb{R}^{C \times H \times W}$. Then, the learned similarity features are concatenated with the original features. Next, we use two 1×1 convolutional operation to get the specific features $f_{MRI\_fusion} \in \mathbb{R}^{C \times H \times W}$ and $f_{PET\_fusion} \in \mathbb{R}^{C \times H \times W}$. Since the MRI and PET data we use have sagittal, coronal and horizontal planes, each direction can play a very important role in the diagnosis task of AD. Therefore, we perform feature learning on the three slices by exchanging the dimensions, and concatenate the three features together. To achieve this, we first swap the dimensions and design three branches, each corresponding to one dimension of feature learning. Along the channel dimension, we use a convolution kernel $k_C \in \mathbb{R}^{1 \times n \times n}$, get the feature $f_C \in \mathbb{R}^{C \times H \times W}$. Along the height dimension, we use the convolution kernel $k_H \in \mathbb{R}^{n \times 1 \times n}$ to get the feature $f_H \in \mathbb{R}^{C \times H \times W}$. Along the width dimension, we use the convolution kernel $k_W \in \mathbb{R}^{n \times n \times 1}$ to get the feature $f_W \in \mathbb{R}^{C \times H \times W}$. Then, the three features are concatenated together to get the final feature $f_{dim} = \{f_C, f_H, f_W\} \in \mathbb{R}^{3C \times H \times W}$. Finally, the number of output channels is reshaped to the number of input channels through a 1×1 convolutional layer.

3.4 Spatial-Channel Attention

In order to accurately diagnose AD, it is very important to learn the spatial features of brain images as well as the channel features. Therefore, we design a spatial-channel attention (SCA) module to further learn the spatial and channel information of high-level features after extracting high-level features, which can improve the performance of our method.

As shown in Fig. 5, our SCA consists of a channel attention branch and a spatial attention branch. In the channel attention branch, the feature maps are first converted into vectors by global average pooling, and then passed through two 1×1 convolutional layer to calculate the weight of each channel, and finally the feature map is the input feature multiplied by the channel weight. In the spatial attention branch, the feature map first averages the channel features, the weight in each pixel is determined by the sigmoid activation function, and finally the feature map is the pixel-wise multiplied weight. Finally, the outputs of the channel and spatial attention branches are added element-wise to form new feature maps.

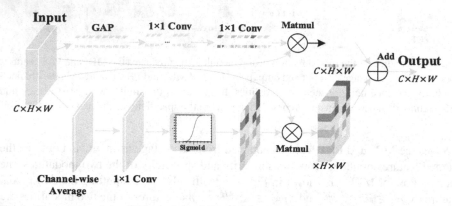

Fig. 5. Illustration of the SCA module. SCA consists of two branches, the channel and spatial attention branch. The two branches learn channel and spatial attention to enhance feature representation.

4   Experiment and Results

4.1   Experiment Settings

To train the proposed model, we screen a total of 560 subjects from ADNI database and divide them into three categories according to their diagnostic results: 144 subjects with AD, 186 subjects with HC, and 230 subjects with MCI. Among them, MCI is further subdivided into 85 progressive MCI (pMCI) subjects and 145 stable MCI (sMCI) subjects according to whether the MCI subjects would transform into AD during the 36-month follow-up process. All subjects screened in this paper have both 3T MRI and PET image data and clinical scores.

For the preprocessing of MRI and PET data, the tools we use mainly include SPM and CAT. We use CAT to preprocess MRI data with the following procedures: 1) noise filtering; 2) resampling; 3) bias field correction; 4) skull stripping; 5) linear registration; 6) tissue segmentation; 7) spatial normalize; 8) clipping boundaries. Compared with MRI, PET data preprocessing has fewer steps, mainly including: 1) registration; 2) spatial normalization; 3) skull stripping; 4) smoothing. All images are preprocessed to $128 \times 128 \times 100$.

We use Pytorch to train the models on a single NVIDIA GPU. During the training process, stochastic gradient descent (SGD) algorithm is used as an optimizer, the momentum constant and weight decay coefficient are respectively set as 0.9 and 0.001. The loss function is cross-entropy, the initial learning rate is set to 10^{-4}. The total epochs are 50, we use cosine annealing algorithm to adjust the learning rate. We also use dropout strategy before the last fully connected layer to overcome the overfitting issue. Since the amount of used data is small, we employ ten-fold cross-validation to train our model.

Table 1. Diagnosis performance of different methods (%).

Task	LKA	SCA	MFFB	ACC	SEN	SPEC	F1	BAC	AUC
AD vs NC				94.24 ± 2.33	95.23 ± 3.94	93.08 ± 5.41	94.91 ± 2.01	94.15 ± 2.45	97.21 ± 1.99
	✓			94.54 ± 3.53	96.95 ± 3.97	92.01 ± 5.20	94.93 ± 3.63	94.48 ± 3.42	96.95 ± 3.28
	✓	✓		95.30 ± 2.58	**97.55 ± 2.52**	92.69 ± 3.96	95.78 ± 2.47	95.12 ± 2.59	97.79 ± 1.31
	✓	✓	✓	**96.21 ± 2.56**	97.41 ± 2.88	**94.64 ± 3.82**	**96.47 ± 2.67**	**96.03 ± 2.60**	**98.16 ± 1.28**
pMCI vs sMCI				80.43 ± 6.45	88.61 ± 8.73	66.29 ± 15.54	84.66 ± 6.55	77.45 ± 7.25	85.45 ± 7.58
	✓			83.26 ± 5.51	89.64 ± 5.31	**72.26 ± 10.93**	86.70 ± 5.33	80.95 ± 5.14	87.45 ± 5.23
	✓	✓		83.91 ± 3.25	88.91 ± 8.99	71.72 ± 18.37	87.04 ± 3.96	80.32 ± 5.94	87.88 ± 4.41
	✓	✓	✓	**83.91 ± 4.37**	**90.70 ± 4.73**	72.00 ± 13.29	**87.70 ± 3.08**	**81.35 ± 6.12**	**88.83 ± 5.23**
pMCI vs NC				87.62 ± 4.85	95.54 ± 6.44	66.92 ± 15.41	91.17 ± 3.69	81.23 ± 6.19	92.02 ± 4.89
	✓			88.56 ± 4.02	**97.75 ± 2.95**	66.37 ± 16.75	92.14 ± 2.50	82.06 ± 7.73	93.94 ± 3.60
	✓	✓		89.48 ± 3.08	96.61 ± 3.08	75.59 ± 13.11	92.57 ± 2.35	**86.10 ± 5.35**	**94.24 ± 2.54**
	✓	✓	✓	**89.66 ± 4.37**	95.19 ± 4.43	**76.80 ± 14.25**	92.50 ± 3.68	85.99 ± 6.60	93.34 ± 4.21
sMCI vs NC				66.92 ± 7.61	**84.96 ± 18.69**	41.00 ± 28.56	**73.19 ± 9.68**	62.98 ± 9.28	68.16 ± 10.01
	✓			67.51 ± 4.87	82.18 ± 19.83	40.97 ± 30.53	72.43 ± 9.27	61.57 ± 7.29	68.22 ± 5.58
	✓	✓		67.53 ± 5.81	81.03 ± 14.73	45.79 ± 24.94	72.97 ± 7.28	63.41 ± 8.00	70.75 ± 6.39
	✓	✓	✓	**67.66 ± 6.09**	78.41 ± 15.69	**50.43 ± 21.70**	72.14 ± 9.40	**64.42 ± 7.42**	**70.77 ± 7.28**

Table 2. Diagnosis performance compared with the state-of-the-art methods (%).

Task	Method	ACC	SEN	SPEC	F1	BAC	AUC
AD vs NC	ResNet50	91.21 ± 2.51	95.97 ± 5.02	85.02 ± 7.07	92.39 ± 2.38	90.49 ± 2.67	95.57 ± 2.18
	ResNet50-D	91.21 ± 3.82	93.92 ± 5.54	87.44 ± 7.51	92.23 ± 3.74	90.68 ± 4.19	95.53 ± 2.59
	EfficientNet	93.03 ± 4.02	95.22 ± 3.26	89.57 ± 10.19	93.75 ± 3.49	92.40 ± 4.38	96.00 ± 2.22
	Mobile-Former	91.21 ± 2.77	95.78 ± 4.66	87.47 ± 6.63	93.02 ± 2.66	91.62 ± 2.91	95.16 ± 1.85
	ViTAEV2	94.54 ± 3.53	96.95 ± 3.97	92.01 ± 5.20	94.93 ± 3.63	94.48 ± 3.42	96.95 ± 3.28
	CoAtNet	95.45 ± 2.03	96.13 ± 5.00	93.16 ± 5.58	95.72 ± 2.42	94.65 ± 2.35	97.26 ± 1.71
	Proposed	**96.21 ± 2.56**	**97.41 ± 2.88**	**94.64 ± 3.82**	**96.47 ± 2.67**	**96.03 ± 2.60**	**98.16 ± 1.28**
pMCI vs sMCI	ResNet50	83.16 ± 4.46	85.42 ± 8.15	75.83 ± 8.63	85.52 ± 5.87	80.63 ± 3.49	87.49 ± 5.10
	ResNet50-D	83.03 ± 5.73	90.03 ± 6.96	66.00 ± 24.03	86.61 ± 5.30	78.02 ± 10.54	87.41 ± 6.55
	EfficientNet	77.17 ± 5.16	82.31 ± 14.07	62.24 ± 21.21	80.87 ± 8.57	72.28 ± 7.40	81.68 ± 8.17
	Mobile-Former	76.95 ± 5.51	88.75 ± 5.24	57.77 ± 16.67	82.97 ± 3.52	73.26 ± 7.15	80.07 ± 6.60
	ViTAEV2	81.73 ± 6.46	**93.69 ± 5.55**	61.85 ± 20.74	86.25 ± 5.17	77.77 ± 8.81	86.12 ± 6.77

(continued)

Table 2. (*continued*)

Task	Method	ACC	SEN	SPEC	F1	BAC	AUC
	CoAtNet	81.95 ± 7.01	88.16 ± 9.89	70.87 ± 14.52	84.70 ± 9.05	79.51 ± 5.69	85.97 ± 9.36
	Proposed	**83.91 ± 4.37**	90.70 ± 4.73	**72.00 ± 13.29**	**87.70 ± 3.08**	**81.35 ± 6.12**	**88.83 ± 5.23**
pMCI vs NC	ResNet50	87.82 ± 2.21	97.43 ± 2.37	63.48 ± 16.49	91.65 ± 1.37	80.46 ± 7.32	92.46 ± 2.49
	ResNet50-D	87.43 ± 3.72	93.07 ± 6.18	73.97 ± 16.93	90.95 ± 2.82	83.52 ± 6.80	91.51 ± 3.42
	EfficientNet	87.47 ± 4.12	96.27 ± 5.14	67.64 ± 14.73	91.19 ± 3.36	81.95 ± 6.61	91.31 ± 3.59
	Mobile-Former	83.81 ± 6.41	95.26 ± 4.75	57.97 ± 17.67	88.90 ± 4.81	76.61 ± 8.20	88.18 ± 8.21
	ViTAEV2	87.25 ± 4.74	94.65 ± 3.44	71.23 ± 11.65	91.03 ± 3.28	82.94 ± 6.32	93.37 ± 4.40
	CoAtNet	87.09 ± 3.45	**96.34 ± 3.25**	65.24 ± 11.71	90.99 ± 2.78	80.79 ± 5.42	93.00 ± 2.75
	Proposed	**89.66 ± 4.37**	95.19 ± 4.43	**76.80 ± 14.25**	**92.50 ± 3.68**	**85.99 ± 6.60**	**93.34 ± 4.21**
sMCI vs NC	ResNet50	62.51 ± 5.39	57.67 ± 22.77	**65.22 ± 21.91**	60.22 ± 15.68	61.44 ± 6.63	63.17 ± 5.33
	ResNet50-D	64.33 ± 8.98	63.35 ± 22.70	62.27 ± 16.26	63.77 ± 15.19	62.81 ± 7.19	65.02 ± 9.86
	EfficientNet	65.38 ± 5.19	77.33 ± 25.19	45.06 ± 25.28	68.12 ± 17.45	61.20 ± 6.39	63.79 ± 4.19
	Mobile-Former	58.13 ± 5.51	61.89 ± 30.59	45.31 ± 30.71	57.10 ± 20.48	53.60 ± 3.78	58.86 ± 8.32
	ViTAEV2	63.15 ± 6.26	63.94 ± 29.43	55.41 ± 29.88	61.07 ± 20.75	59.67 ± 5.75	64.34 ± 8.53
	CoAtNet	64.66 ± 6.58	73.31 ± 15.13	51.72 ± 17.51	69.12 ± 9.45	62.52 ± 6.35	66.86 ± 8.87
	Proposed	**67.66 ± 6.09**	**78.41 ± 15.69**	50.43 ± 21.70	**72.14 ± 9.40**	**64.42 ± 7.42**	**70.77 ± 7.28**

4.2 Diagnosis Performance and Discussion

In this paper, we only perform binary diagnosis tasks, in which AD, pMCI and sMCI are detected from NC, respectively. Table 1 shows the results of our model. For convenience, we highlight the best result in boldface. Table 1 suggests that we achieve an accuracy of 94.24%, 80.43%, 87.62% and 66.92% by merely using the baseline model on the four classification tasks. After adding the attention mechanism, the performance is significantly improved, which indicates the effectiveness of using large convolution kernels to generate attention maps. We further utilize SCA in our model, and the performance is significantly further improved to 95.30%, 83.91%, 89.48% and 67.53%. Of course, the best performing models are built with LKA, SCA and MFFB. Performance comparisons on the four tasks demonstrate the effectiveness of the modules we use. We further compare our method with other CNNs as well as CNN-Transformer hybrid methods. As shown in Table 2, the proposed method achieves the best accuracy of 96.12% on AD and NC tasks, which is 5% better than ResNet50 and Mobile-Former. In addition, our model achieves the best performance on three other tasks, among which it outperforms Mobile-Former by 9.53% on the task of sMCI vs NC.

The results on the four classification tasks illustrate that our method can effectively diagnose AD. Figure 6 shows the receiver operating characteristic (ROC) curve and the area under the curve (AUC). On the four tasks, the ROC curves obtained by our method are the best, which further illustrates the effectiveness of our method.

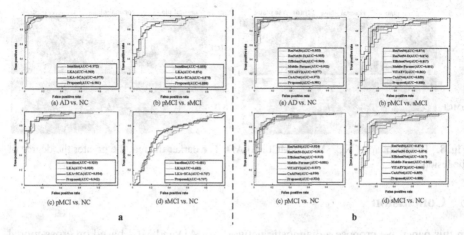

(a) AD vs. NC	(b) pMCI vs. sMCI	(a) AD vs. NC	(b) pMCI vs. sMCI
(c) pMCI vs. NC	(d) sMCI vs. NC	(c) pMCI vs. NC	(d) sMCI vs. NC
a		b	

Fig. 6. ROC curves of different methods. Red: our proposed method, the ROC curves obtained by our method are all optimal, illustrating the effectiveness of our method. (Color figure online)

4.3 t-SNE Visualization and Heatmap

t-SNE is an algorithm for dimensionality reduction of high-dimensional data. All test data are reduced to 2D using t-SNE, and the data distribution can then be visualized visually. Figure 7 shows the results for AD versus NC, pMCI versus sMCI, pMCI versus NC, and sMCI versus NC. The blue dots represent NC subjects, and red dots represent AD, pMCI, and sMCI subjects. In AD vs. NC task and pMCI vs. NC task, there is a clear dividing line between the distributions of different categories of features extracted by this method. However, the distributive clustering effect of the extracted different-class features in the classification task of sMCI vs NC is poor, which indicates the direction of improvement of our method. Figure 7 shows that the proposed CNN-Transformer architecture can learn the most discriminative features. At the same time, we also drew a heat map. In the heat map, the darker the red, the deeper the lesion. From the heat map, we can see that from NC to AD, the color of the brain area is getting deeper and deeper, which indicates that the degree of lesions is getting bigger and bigger. The red areas in Fig. 8 coincide with the brain's hippocampus, amygdala, thalamus, and ventricles, which are reported to be responsible for short-term memory and the early stages of AD.

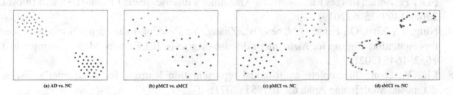

| (a) AD vs. NC | (b) pMCI vs. sMCI | (c) pMCI vs. NC | (d) sMCI vs. NC |

Fig. 7. t-SNE visualization. In the (a), (c) and (d), blue represents NC, and red represents AD, pMCI, and sMCI, respectively. In the (b), blue represents sMCI, and red represents pMCI.

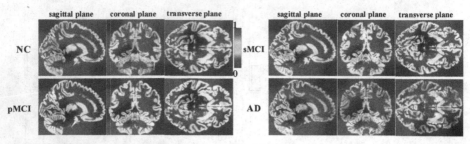

Fig. 8. The heatmap of NC, sMCI, pMCI and AD. The darker the red, the greater the degree of the lesion.

5   Conclusion

In this paper, we propose a diagnostic network for AD and MCI based on cross-modal feature fusion. Experiments demonstrate that our model leads to the best diagnosis performance compared to the state-of-the-art methods. In the future, we will try to explore more deep learning methods to detect early stage of AD, especially its prodromal stage, MCI (i.e., sMCI and pMCI). Besides, we will also try to study more useful fusion way between MRI and PET modalities.

References

1. Gauthier, R.-N.P., Morais, S.J.A., Webster, C.: World Alzheimer Report 2021. Alzheimer's Disease International, Journey through the diagnosis of dementia, London, England (2021)
2. Guan, H., Liu, Y., Yang, E., Yap, P.T., Shen, D., Liu, M.: Multi-site MRI harmonization via attention-guided deep domain adaptation for brain disorder identification. Med. Image Anal. **71**, 102076 (2021)
3. Lao, H., Zhang, X.: Regression and classification of Alzheimer's disease diagnosis using NMF-TDNet features from 3D brain MR image. IEEE J. Biomed. Health Inform. **26**(3), 1103–1115 (2022)
4. Lian, C., Liu, M., Pan, Y., Shen, D.: Attention-guided hybrid network for dementia diagnosis with structural MR images. IEEE Trans. Cybern. **52**(4), 1992–2003 (2022)
5. Pan, X., et al.: Multi-view separable pyramid network for AD prediction at MCI stage by (18)F-FDG brain PET imaging. IEEE Trans. Med. Imaging **40**(1), 81–92 (2021)
6. Pan, X., Adel, M., Fossati, C., Gaidon, T., Guedj, E.: Multilevel feature representation of FDG-PET brain images for diagnosing Alzheimer's disease. IEEE J Biomed. Health Inform. **23**(4), 1499–1506 (2019)
7. Ning, Z., Xiao, Q., Feng, Q., Chen, W., Zhang, Y.: Relation-induced multi-modal shared representation learning for Alzheimer's disease diagnosis. IEEE Trans. Med. Imaging **40**(6), 1632–1645 (2021)
8. Liu, Y., et al.: Incomplete multi-modal representation learning for Alzheimer's disease diagnosis. Med. Image Anal. **69**, 101953 (2021)
9. Zhang, J., Liu, M., Le, A., Gao, Y., Shen, D.: Alzheimer's disease diagnosis using landmark-based features from longitudinal structural MR images. IEEE J. Biomed. Health Inform. **21**(6), 1607–1616 (2017)
10. Chollet, F.: Xception: deep learning with depthwise separable convolutions. In: 2017 IEEE Conference on Computer Vision and Pattern Recognition (CVPR), pp. 1800–1807 (2017)

11. Graham, B., et al.: LeViT: a vision transformer in ConvNet's clothing for faster inference. In: 2021 IEEE/CVF International Conference on Computer Vision (ICCV), Montreal,Canada, pp. 12239–12249 (2021)

12. Sandler, M., Howard, A., Zhu, M., Zhmoginov, A., Chen, L.-C.: MobileNetV2: inverted residuals and linear bottlenecks. In: 2018 IEEE/CVF Conference on Computer Vision and Pattern Recognition, Salt Lake City, USA, pp. 4510–4520 (2018)

13. Tan, M., Le, Q.V.: MixConv: mixed depthwise convolutional kernels. In: 2019 British Machine Vision Conference, Cardiff, Wales, UK, pp. 116.111–116.113 (2019). https://doi.org/10.5244/C.33.116

14. Dosovitskiy, A., et al.: An image is worth 16x16 words: Transformers for image recognition at scale. arXiv preprint arXiv:2010.11929 (2020)

15. Wang, F., et al.: Residual attention network for image classification. In: 2017 IEEE Conference on Computer Vision and Pattern Recognition (CVPR), Salt Lake City, USA, pp. 6450–6458 (2017)

16. Hu, J., Shen, L., Albanie, S., Sun, G., Vedaldi, A.: Gather-excite: exploiting feature context in convolutional neural networks. In: Proceedings of the 32nd International Conference on Neural Information Processing Systems, Montréal, Canada, pp. 9423–9433 (2018)

Topological Data Analysis for Biomedical Imaging

Future Unruptured Intracranial Aneurysm Growth Prediction Using Mesh Convolutional Neural Networks

Kimberley M. Timmins[1]([✉]), Maarten J. Kamphuis[2], Iris N. Vos[1], Birgitta K. Velthuis[2], Irene C. van der Schaaf[2], and Hugo J. Kuijf[1]

[1] Image Sciences Institute, University Medical Center Utrecht, Utrecht, The Netherlands
k.m.timmins@umcutrecht.nl
[2] Department of Radiology, University Medical Center Utrecht, Utrecht, The Netherlands

Abstract. The growth of unruptured intracranial aneurysms (UIAs) is a predictor of rupture. Therefore, for further imaging surveillance and treatment planning, it is important to be able to predict if an UIA is likely to grow based on an initial baseline Time-of-Flight MRA (TOF-MRA). It is known that the size and shape of UIAs are predictors of aneurysm growth and/or rupture. We perform a feasibility study of using a mesh convolutional neural network for future UIA growth prediction from baseline TOF-MRAs. We include 151 TOF-MRAs, with 169 UIAs where 49 UIAs were classified as growing and 120 as stable, based on the clinical definition of growth (>1 mm increase in size in follow-up scan). UIAs were segmented from TOF-MRAs and meshes were automatically generated. We investigate the input of both UIA mesh only and region-of-interest (ROI) meshes including UIA and surrounding parent vessels. We develop a classification model to predict UIAs that will grow or remain stable. The model consisted of a mesh convolutional neural network including additional novel input edge features of shape index and curvedness which describe the surface topology. It was investigated if input edge mid-point co-ordinates influenced the model performance. The model with highest AUC (63.8%) for growth prediction was using UIA meshes with input edge mid-point co-ordinate features (average F1 score = 62.3%, accuracy = 66.9%, sensitivity = 57.3%, specificity = 70.8%). We present a future UIA growth prediction model based on a mesh convolutional neural network with promising results.

Keywords: Meshes · Aneurysms · Growth prediction · Geometric deep learning · Topology

1 Introduction

Approximately 3% of the general population has a unruptured intracranial aneurysm (UIAs) [5]. If an UIA ruptures, it leads to subarachnoid haemorrhage

---

I. C. van der Schaaf and H. J. Kuijf—Joint last author.

J. S. H. Baxter et al. (Eds.): EPIMI 2022/ML-CDS 2022/TDA4BiomedicalImaging 2022,
LNCS 13755, pp. 103–112, 2022.
https://doi.org/10.1007/978-3-031-23223-7_9

with a high mortality and morbidity rate. Neurosurgical or endovascular treatment can prevent UIAs from rupture, but carry a considerable risk. Therefore a balanced decision based on the rupture and treatment complication risk must be made [1]. UIA growth is an important rupture risk factor [9], and if detected, preventative treatment should be considered. Most UIAs are monitored, using Time-of-Flight Magnetic Resonance Angiographs (TOF-MRAs) or Computed Tomography Angiographs (CTAs). Currently, 2D size measurements of the UIAs are made and an aneurysm will be considered to be growing if there is a change in size (>1 mm) [6]. UIA shape is also known to be different in aneurysms that grow [2]. The ELAPSS score [2] is a clinical score for UIA growth prediction based on patient and aneurysm characteristics. The predictors are: Earlier subarachnoid hemorrhage, aneurysm Location, Age, Population, aneurysm Size and Shape. Shape is assessed visually as 'Regular' or 'Irregular'.

As computer-aided radiology tools continue to be developed, 3D volume and morphology measurements of UIAs can be made [19], including to distinguish between growing and stable aneurysms [12,13,22]. UIA rupture risk prediction models have been developed based on morphological parameters, as well as classical parameters [10,14]. More recently, some prediction models for aneurysmal stability and growth have been proposed [3,15].

Liu et al. [15] investigated predicting aneurysm stability using machine learning regression models and 12 morphology radiomics features. The dataset included 420 aneurysms (4–8 mm). Instability was defined as ruptured within a month, growth or adjacent structure compressive symptoms. They determined flatness to be the most important morphological predictor of aneurysm stability. Bizjak et al. [3] found using point clouds with PointNet++ for future UIA growth prediction had a higher accuracy than other machine learning models based on morphological parameters. The method was performed using only 44 UIAs, where 25 growing and 19 stable. UIAs were visually inspected in 3D to be classified as growing or stable.

Various different morphology measurements and definitions of growth or stability have been used in these studies, making it difficult to make direct comparisons. However, it is clear that UIA shape and surface topology is an important predictor of future UIA growth and that deep learning methods may have an advantage over using predefined morphology parameters. Geometric deep learning methods are well suited to this problem, as they accurately describe the shape and topology of a surface by using point clouds or meshes [4]. Meshes may have a preference over point clouds as they include connectivity information, providing more information about the surface topology. Segmented UIA meshes could be used as we already know UIA shape is a growth predictor growth. Alternatively, parent vessels in a Region-of-Interest (ROI) around the UIA could be used which includes UIA-vessel configuration and exact UIA segmentation is not required.

MeshCNN [7] is a convolutional neural network (CNN) developed for classification and segmentation problems using 3D triangular meshes. Convolutions and pooling are performed on edges of the meshes, based on an edge neighbourhood. Five relative scale, translation and rotation invariant geometric edge are determined for each edge as input features for the model. These five geometric features are: the dihedral angle, two inner angles and two edge-length ratios. MeshCNN has only been used for a few medical imaging classification and segmentation problems, including age prediction based on the neonatal white matter cortical surface [24] and UIA segmentation from a parent vessel [18]. In our previous work, we proposed a modified version of MeshCNN for UIA detection based on brain vessel surface meshes [20].

In this paper, we propose a prediction model for future UIA growth from baseline TOF-MRAs using a mesh convolutional neural network. We investigate the use of meshes of UIAs alone, and region-of-interest (ROI) meshes including the UIA with parent vessels as input for these models and their performance for future UIA growth prediction. We also investigate the addition of edge midpoint co-ordinate input features of the meshes and the impact on the model performance.

2 Materials and Methods

2.1 Dataset

The dataset consisted of 151 baseline Time-of-Flight MRAs (TOF-MRAs) taken from routine clinical scans. We included patients with UIAs who met the following inclusion criteria: 1) A TOF-MRA or CTA was available at baseline and follow-up, 2) the follow-up scan was performed at least 6 months after the baseline scan, and 3) the patient had at least 1 untreated UIA present on both baseline and follow-up imaging. The most recent follow-up scan in which the UIA remained untreated and unruptured was used for growth assessment. Fusiform and ruptured aneurysms were excluded. All scans were made from the University Medical Center Utrecht between 2006 and 2020. The average time between baseline and follow-up scans was 5.2 ± 3.3 years (range: 1–16 years) The mean baseline aneurysm size was 5.0 ± 2.2 mm with a range of 1.3–14.7 mm. Manual 2D length and width UIA measurements were performed in IntelliSpace Portal (Philips Healthcare) by an experienced neuro-radiologist (I.C.v.d.S.) and a trained PhD-student (M.J.K.) according to standard clinical protocol. Growth was defined as a ≥ 1.0 mm increase in any direction between the baseline and follow-up scan [6]. Based on this definition, UIAs were categorised as either 'growing' (30%, n = 49) or 'stable' (70%, n = 120).

2.2 Methods

Input Mesh Generation. All baseline TOF-MRAs were pre-processed using an N4 bias field correction algorithm and z-score normalised before being resampled to have voxel size 0.357 mm × 0.357 mm × 0.500 mm (median of the dataset). All UIA and ROI selection, mesh generation and processing was performed completely automatically based on UIA annotations.

UIA Mesh Generation. UIA meshes were generated and pre-processed auto-matically based on the TOF-MRAs and UIA annotations. UIAs were manually segmented from the TOF-MRAs using annotations drawn on axial slices in in-house-developed software implemented in MeVisLab (MeVis Medical Solutions) (performed by I.C.v.d.S. and M.J.K). A triangular mesh was automatically fit-ted to the outside of the UIA surface using a Marching Cubes algorithm [17]. All UIA meshes were down-sampled to 1000 edges and included just the UIA and no other vessels.

Region-of-Interest (ROI) Mesh Generation. ROI meshes were automatically gen-erated from the TOF-MRAs using the UIA segmentations. An existing 3D U-net was used to automatically perform full vessel segmentation from the scans [23]. Based on the UIA segmentation, a region-of-interest (ROI) including only the UIA and parent vessels was made. The centre-of-mass of the UIA segmentation was determined and the ROI included all connected vessels (and UIA) within a 20 mm cube around the centre-of-mass. A mesh was automatically fitted to the outside of the UIA and parent vessel surface using a Marching Cubes algorithm [17]. All ROI meshes were down-sampled to 2000 edges.

Input Edge Features. Based on the generated UIA and ROI meshes, new input edge features were automatically determined per edge. These were shape index, curvedness and edge mid-point co-ordinates. These further edge features (shape index, curvedness and mid-point co-ordinates) could then be included as input to the network, in addition to the original five geometric edge features.

Shape index and curvedness are rotation and translation invariant measures which describe the topology of the UIA surface. The invariant nature of these novel input edge features ideal for use in MeshCNN. It is known from our previ-ous work in UIA detection that the addition of both shape index and curvedness as input edge features improve the performance of the original MeshCNN [21]. Shape descriptor values; shape index and curvedness, were calculated for each vertex on the mesh surface using the standard formulae [11]. An edge was then given a shape descriptor value (shape index or curvedness), as being the average of the values at the corresponding end vertices of the edge.

The addition of edge mid-point co-ordinate values was suggested in the orig-inal MeshCNN paper [7]. We experiment with including these co-ordinates in our models as we know location is important as an aneurysm growth predictor [2]. Edge mid-point co-ordinates (x, y, z) were determined as the average of the world co-ordinates of the corresponding end vertices of the edge.

Figure 1 shows an example generation of a ROI mesh including shape index values determined for each edge.

Model Implementation. A ConvNet style network was set up based on our modified MeshCNN framework [20] including four convolutional layers and four pooling layers. Four different model configurations were investigated. The first model (uia_model) had UIA meshes only as input, with 1000 edges. Pooling layer

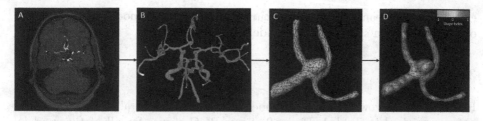

Fig. 1. Example generation of input region-of-interest (ROI) mesh including parent vessels and UIA. A: TOF-MRA with annotated UIA shown overlaid in red. B: Vessel segmentation performed using 3D U-net [23]. C: ROI selection including UIA and parent vessels, followed by mesh generation. D: Shape index determination for each edge, to be used as an additional input feature alongside curvedness and edge coordinates (Color figure online).

configuration for the UIA model was: 750, 600, 500, 400. The second model (roi_model) had ROI meshes including UIA and parent vessels as input. The pooling layer configuration for the ROI model was: 1500, 1200, 1000, 800. All models were made to include shape index and curvedness as additional input features to the original five edge geometric features of MeshCNN. This meant that there were seven input edge features as standard. For each different input, two models were trained. The first with the seven input edge features (uia_model_1, roi_model_1), and the second including edge mid-point co-ordinates (x, y, z) as further additional input features (uia_model_2, roi_model_2), meaning there were ten input edge features. No augmentation was used.

For all models, all other hyperparameters were kept the same, and as similar to the original paper as possible [7]. Both a weighted data sampler and weighted cross-entropy loss function were used, based on the class distribution of growing and stable UIAs (0.7 to growing, 0.3 to stable). Batch normalisation was used with a batch size of 50 meshes and a learning rate of 0.0002. The classification model was trained to predict future growth of the UIA as defined by the clinical definition, whereby output was one of the two classes: growing or stable. All experiments were performed using five-fold cross-validation where the validation splits were made randomly and kept the same for each experiment. The models were trained for a maximum of 200 epochs with validation every 5 epochs and the model with the highest average F1 score for each split was selected. The model was implemented in Python 3.8.5 with Pytorch version 1.8.0 on a NVIDIA TITAN X Pascal (12 GB) GPU with CUDA version 11.2.

For final model assessment, we determined the classification accuracy, growth prediction sensitivity and specificity, where the metrics were averaged across all validation splits. A true positive was considered a correctly identified growing UIA, a true negative was a correctly identified stable UIA. Sensitivity and Specificity were determined using these definitions, therefore high sensitivity suggests the model is good at detecting growing UIAs and high specificity suggests the model is good at detecting stable UIAs. We plotted the mean ROC curve and calculated the mean area under the curve (AUC) for each model, as the average over all validation splits for each model.

3   Results

Results of the growth prediction models averaged across all validation splits are summarised in Table 1. Figure 2 shows ROC curves for all of the models. Roi_model_1, using ROI meshes and no edge mid-point co-ordinates, had the highest accuracy (0.761), F1 score (0.681) and specificity (0.883) suggesting it performs optimally for stable aneurysm detection. Uia_model_2, using UIA meshes and including edge mid-point co-ordinates, had the highest sensitivity for growth detection. Overall, both the second models including edge mid-point co-ordinates had higher AUC and sensitivity values but slightly lower accuracy and F1 scores.

Table 1. Classification metrics for each model. F1 score is the average of F1 score for each class (growing and stable). A true positive was considered a correctly identified growing UIA, a true negative was a correctly identified stable UIA. Sensitivity and Specificity were determined using these definitions. AUC is the area under the mean ROC curve in Fig. 2. Values are provided as mean (standard deviation) across all validation splits (standard deviation)

Model	Accuracy	F1 score	Sensitivity	Specificity	AUC
uia_model_1	0.704 (0.077)	0.617 (0.062)	0.389 (0.048)	0.833 (0.121)	0.620 (0.119)
uia_model_2	0.669 (0.061)	0.623 (0.073)	0.573 (0.155)	0.708 (0.075)	0.638 (0.116)
roi_model_1	0.761 (0.017)	0.681 (0.021)	0.458 (0.038)	0.883 (0.030)	0.606 (0.056)
roi_model_2	0.713 (0.075)	0.650 (0.077)	0.498 (0.090)	0.781 (0.110)	0.622 (0.064)

4   Discussion

In this paper, we demonstrate that a future UIA growth prediction model could be developed using a mesh convolutional neural network, which considers the topology of UIAs and their parent vasculature. We found that adding edge mid-point co-ordinates as input features to the network increases the AUC and sensitivity of growth prediction but reduces the overall accuracy of the model (uia_model_2, roi_model_2). Using ROI meshes as opposed to UIA meshes alone, improved the accuracy and F1 score of the model but has a decreased AUC for growth prediction. A sensitive growth prediction model should consider using UIA meshes as input and including edge mid-point co-ordinates as input features (uia_model_2).

We found using UIA meshes alone (uia_model_2) improved the AUC relative to using the ROI including parent vessels (roi_model_2). This suggests that it is the topology of the aneurysm surface itself which is high indicative of growth or

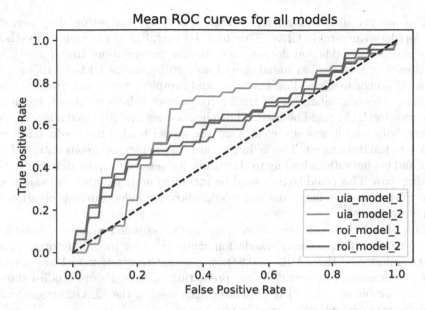

Fig. 2. ROC curves of all trained models for growth prediction classification. Each line is the mean of the performance across all cross validation splits for each model. The black dotted line indicates a classifier which would give random choice.

stability as opposed to UIA configuration relative to parent vessels. This result is similar to previous studies, where measurements of just the UIA distinguish growing and stable UIAs [12,13,22]. However, it is worth noting that using a ROI as opposed to the UIA mesh does not greatly reduce the performance of the method. A ROI mesh, is easier to achieve in the clinic as it requires only a click of a centre point to select the ROI. Whereas, currently the UIA meshes require accurate manual UIA segmentation. Therefore, a ROI model have more clinic applicability and has adequate performance for UIA growth prediction.

The inclusion of input edge mid-point co-ordinate features increased the AUC and growth prediction sensitivity. This is likely because the co-ordinate provides aneurysm location information to the network. Location is a known predictor of growth [2]. In the original MeshCNN paper [7] it was commented that adding in edge co-ordinates reduced the model performance, possibly due to removing the rotation, translation and uniform scaling in-variance of the usual relative geometric input edge features. However, in real-life applications, such as in medical images, the co-ordinates give important information about the location of lesions. Therefore, the addition of these features only appears to improve the performance in this scenario. Further studies could investigate the use of relative position input features, to ensure the in-variance to rotation, translation and scaling is kept. Another possibility could be to include position/location, and potentially other known growth predictors, as global features in the final layers of the network.

The models all had a relatively high specificity, suggesting they perform well for detecting stable UIAs. This may be useful in clinic to identify those UIAs which are stable and do not need further investigation. In our study, we had a relatively large class imbalance of only 30% growing UIAs to 70% stable UIAs. Although weighted loss functions and samplers were used, this does not eliminate the class imbalance. In the future, a more balanced dataset, including more growing UIAs could be used. The validation results displayed a large range in sensitivity, and it was also clear, that the model tended to over-fit relatively quickly to the training set. This is due, in part, to the heterogeneous nature of the UIAs and configurations leading to the validation sets being quite different to the training data. This could be improved by including more training and validation data. Furthermore, a larger dataset would allow for independent evaluation on a separate test set.

The ELAPSS growth prediction score was determined to have a c-statistic (AUC) of 0.69 in an external validation study [8]. Our model performed only slightly inferior to this (AUC = 0.64), suggesting that our model has comparable performance to current clinical prediction models. Future studies should consider combining the patient characteristics used in the ELAPSS score, with the aneurysm characteristics used in our model.

Our proposed method did not perform as well as the method using Point-Net++ put forward by Bizjak [3] (accuracy = 82%). This may be for a variety of reasons. Firstly, our dataset was imbalanced (30% growing, 70% stable) compared to the dataset they used which included more growing than stable aneurysms. Secondly, in Bizjak et al. they assess growth visually on the pre-processed 3D meshes. Instead, our model can provide a prediction for growth as is currently clinically assessed and accepted in the clinic. Future studies should investigate different definitions of growth, and as computer aided tools for UIA diagnosis and assessment continue to be developed and improve, a definition for volumetric growth should be considered [16,19]. It is difficult to make a comparison of our model to the study by Liu et al. [15] as they are predicting aneurysm stability, which included rupture and not just growth. Furthermore, they have a larger dataset of all aneurysms larger than 4 mm. However, future studies could investigate if our mesh based model could also predict rupture/aneurysm instability as well as growth.

In our previous paper [20], we demonstrated the mesh convolutional neural networks could be used for a modality independent UIA detection method. Based on these results, we believe that our growth prediction method could also be modality independent. This would be helpful in the clinic, where UIAs are often assessed or followed-up with different modalities such as CTA or DSA.

5   Conclusion

We present a future UIA growth prediction model using a mesh convolutional neural network. We demonstrate that both UIA and ROI meshes can be used as input for such a prediction model, and that edge mid-point co-ordinates improve the growth prediction sensitivity. This model may have potential clinical use as an aid for radiologists assessing potential future UIA growth.

Acknowledgements. We acknowledge the support from the Netherlands Cardiovascular Research Initiative: An initiative with support of the Dutch Heart Foundation, CVON2015-08 ERASE and CVON2018-02 ANEURYSM@RISK.

References

1. Algra, A.M., et al.: Procedural clinical complications, case-fatality risks, and risk factors in endovascular and neurosurgical treatment of unruptured intracranial aneurysms: a systematic review and meta-analysis. JAMA Neurol. **76**(3), 282–293 (2019). https://doi.org/10.1001/jamaneurol.2018.4165
2. Backes, D., et al.: ELAPSS score for prediction of risk of growth of unruptured intracranial aneurysms. Neurology **88**(17), 1600–1606 (2017). https://doi.org/10.1212/WNL.0000000000003865
3. Bizjak, Z., Pernus, F., Spiclin, Z.: Deep shape features for predicting future intracranial aneurysm growth. Front. Physiol. **12**(July), 1–10 (2021). https://doi.org/10.3389/fphys.2021.644349
4. Cao, W., Yan, Z., He, Z., He, Z.: A comprehensive survey on geometric deep learning. IEEE Access **8**, 35929–35949 (2020), https://doi.org/10.1109/ACCESS.2020.2975067, https://ieeexplore.ieee.org/document/9003285/
5. Greving, J.P., et al.: Development of the PHASES score for prediction of risk of rupture of intracranial aneurysms: a pooled analysis of six prospective cohort studies. Lancet Neurol. **13**(1), 59–66 (2014). https://doi.org/10.1016/S1474-4422(13)70263-1
6. Hackenberg, K.A.M., et al.: Definition and prioritization of data elements for cohort studies and clinical trials on patients with unruptured intracranial aneurysms: proposal of a multidisciplinary research group. Neurocrit. Care **30**(1), 87–101 (2019). https://doi.org/10.1007/s12028-019-00729-0
7. Hanocka, R.: MeshCNN: a network with an edge. ACM Trans. Graph. **38**(4), 1–12 (2019). https://doi.org/10.1145/3306346.3322959
8. van Kammen, M.S., et al.: External validation of the ELAPSS score for prediction of unruptured intracranial aneurysm growth risk. Journal of Stroke **21**(3), 340–346 (2019). https://doi.org/10.5853/jos.2019.01277, http://jstroke.org/journal/view.php?doi=10.5853/jos.2019.01277
9. van der Kamp, L.T., et al.: Risk of rupture after intracranial aneurysm growth. JAMA Neurol. **78**(10), 1228–1235 (2021), https://doi.org/10.1001/jamaneurol.2021.2915, https://jamanetwork.com/journals/jamaneurology/fullarticle/2783663
10. Kim, H.C., et al.: Machine learning application for rupture risk assessment in small-sized intracranial aneurysm. J. Clin. Med. **8**(5), 683 (2019). https://doi.org/10.3390/jcm8050683
11. Koenderink, J., Doorn, A.: Surface shape and curvature scales. Image Vis. Comput. **10**(8), 557–564 (1992)
12. Leemans, E.L., Cornelissen, B.M., Slump, C.H., Majoie, C.B., Cebral, J.R., Marquering, H.A.: Comparing morphology and hemodynamics of stable-versus-growing and grown intracranial aneurysms. Am. J. Neuroradiol. **40**(12), 2102–2110 (2019). https://doi.org/10.3174/ajnr.A6307

13. Leemans, E.L., et al.: Intracranial aneurysm growth: consistency of mor-phological changes. Neurosurg. Focus **47**(1), E5 (2019). https://doi.org/10.3171/2019.4.FOCUS1987, https://thejns.org/view/journals/neurosurg-focus/47/1/article-pE5.xml
14. Prediction of rupture risk in anterior communicating artery aneurysms with a feed-forward artificial neural network. Eur. Radiol. **28**(8), 3268–3275 (2018). https://doi.org/10.1007/s00330-017-5300-3
15. Liu, Q., et al.: Prediction of aneurysm stability using a machine learning model based on PyRadiomics-derived morphological features. Stroke **50**(9), 2314–2321 (2019). https://doi.org/10.1161/STROKEAHA.119.025777
16. Liu, X., et al.: A volumetric metric for monitoring intracranial aneurysms: repeata-bility and growth criteria in a longitudinal MR imaging study. Am. J. Neuroradiol. **42**, 1591–1597 (2021). https://doi.org/10.3174/ajnr.A7190, http://www.ajnr.org/lookup/doi/10.3174/ajnr.A7190
17. Lorensen, W.E., Cline, H.E.: Marching cubes: a high resolution 3D surface con-struction algorithm. ACM Siggraph Comput. Graph. **21**(4), 163–169 (1987)
18. Schneider, L., Niemann, A., Beuing, O., Preim, B., Saalfeld, S.: MedmeshCNN - Enabling meshcnn for medical surface models. Comput. Methods Programs Biomed. **210**, 106372 (2021). https://doi.org/10.1016/j.cmpb.2021.106372, http://arxiv.org/abs/2009.04893
19. Timmins, K.M., et al.: Reliability and agreement of 2D and 3D measurements on MRAS for growth assessment of unruptured intracranial aneurysms. Am. J. Neuro-radiol. **42**(9), 1598–1603 (2021). https://doi.org/10.3174/ajnr.A7186, http://www.ajnr.org/lookup/doi/10.3174/ajnr.A7186
20. Timmins, K.M., Schaaf, I.C., Vos, I.N., Ruigrok, Y.M., Velthuis, B.K., Kuijf, H.J.: Deep learning with vessel surface meshes for intracranial aneurysm detection. In: Iftekharuddin, K.M., Drukker, K., Mazurowski, M.A., Lu, H., Muramatsu, C., Samala, R.K. (eds.) Medical Imaging 2022: Computer-Aided Diagnosis. p. 110. SPIE (2022). https://doi.org/10.1117/12.2610745, https://www.spiedigitallibrary.org/conference-proceedings-of-spie/12033/2610745/Deep-learning-with-vessel-surface-meshes-for-intracranial-aneurysm-detection/10.1117/12.2610745.full
21. Timmins, K.M., van der Schaaf, I.C., Vos, I.N., Ruigrok, Y.M., Velthuis, B.K., Kuijf, H.J.: Geometric deep learning using vascular surface meshes for modality-independent unruptured intracranial aneurysm detection. Under Review (2022)
22. Timmins, K., Kuijf, H., Vergouwen, M., Ruigrok, Y., Velthuis, B., van der Schaaf, I.: Relationship between 3D Morphologic Change and 2D and 3D Growth of Unruptured Intracranial Aneurysms. Am. J. Neuroradiol. **43**, 416–421 (2022). https://doi.org/10.3174/ajnr.A7418, http://www.ajnr.org/lookup/doi/10.3174/ajnr.A7418
23. de Vos, V., Timmins, K., van der Schaaf, I., Ruigrok, Y., Velthuis, B., Kuijf, H.J.: Automatic cerebral vessel extraction in TOF-MRA using deep learning (February 2021), p. 83 (2021). https://doi.org/10.1117/12.2581226
24. Vosylius, V.: Geometric deep learning for post-menstrual age prediction based on the neonatal white matter cortical surface. In: Sudre, C.H., et al. (eds.) UNSURE/GRAIL -2020. LNCS, vol. 12443, pp. 174–186. Springer, Cham (2020). https://doi.org/10.1007/978-3-030-60365-6_17

TDA-Clustering Strategies for the Characterization of Brain Organoids

Clara Brémond-Martin[1,2] ⓘ, Camille Simon-Chane[1(✉)] ⓘ,
Cédric Clouchoux[2] ⓘ, and Aymeric Histace[1] ⓘ

[1] ETIS Laboratory UMR 8051, CY Cergy Paris Université, ENSEA, CNRS,
6 Avenue du Ponceau, 95000 Cergy, France
`camille.simon-chane@ensea.fr`
[2] Witsee, 33 Av. des Champs-Élysées, 75008 Paris, France

Abstract. We propose to use Topological Data Analysis (TDA) to characterize the morphological development of brain organoids. We combine TDA with clustering strategies to characterize the morphology of three developmental stages of segmented brain organoid images. We calculate a linear regression of the H1 feature diagrams as well as entropy, dispersion, and average persistence of H0 and H1 features separately for each developmental stage. We also compute pairwise average Wasserstein distances between features, and within and inter clusters for each developmental stage. To explore all feature vectors from each group, we calculate K-L divergence on the t-SNE reduction of the TDA results.

Early stages are characterized by a persistence diagram with a low slope and intercept, a high entropy within features, and a high Wasserstein distance between clusters near and far from the origin. The opposite is true for later stages. K-L divergences are particularly high between mid-stages and early or late stages, and punctually between some clusters. Results highlight specific morphological patterns at 14 days, corresponding to neuroepithelial formations.

Keywords: Brain organoid · Characterisation · TDA-clustering

1   Introduction

Brain organoids are three dimensional cultures generated in vitro which partially replicate the early development of the human brain. These cultures can mimic brain components such as cortical, ventricular, plexus-choroid or retinal regions. Brain organoids were created for the first time in 2013 and have since given hope to neurobiologists that they can provide in vitro human brain models. However, they suffer from batch-syndrome: in the same culture environment, different brain organoids develop varying numbers and types of structures [16]. To characterize the development of these brain cultures, neurobiologists calculate morphological parameters such as the overall area, perimeter or thickness of

© The Author(s), under exclusive license to Springer Nature Switzerland AG 2022
J. S. H. Baxter et al. (Eds.): EPIMI 2022/ML-CDS 2022/TDA4BiomedicalImaging 2022,
LNCS 13755, pp. 113–122, 2022.
https://doi.org/10.1007/978-3-031-23223-7_10

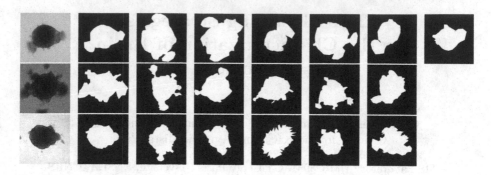

Fig. 1. Dataset of binary images on which the TDA is performed. A sample organoid from [14] is given for each developmental stage. All input segmentation masks are shown. First row: 9 days. Second row: 14 days. Third row: 15 days.

certain structures. This task is tedious and time consuming since it is most often performed manually or using generic semi-automatic software that is not adapted to the various shapes of brain organoids [5].

Our aim is to develop a clustering solution to help neurobiologists automatically characterize their images and recognize their developmental stage. We use Topological Data Analysis (TDA) to infer high dimensional structures from low dimensional representations to assemble discrete points into global structures such as persistence diagrams. TDA, increasingly used in the biomedical domain, converts the original data into global topological objects [23].

In a previous study, brain organoid shapes were extracted from bright-field images using a U-Net segmentation algorithm with various data augmentation strategies [6]. Here we propose to characterize the developmental stage of segmented brain organoids images with TDA and TDA-clustering. As a new analysis method for these biological images, we combined TDA with Kmeans and SVM to group features within each diagram. We pave the way to identify the developmental stage of these cultures by using TDA as a predictive solution.

2 Methods

2.1 Resources

We consider 19 binary images (250×250 pixels), shown Fig. 1. They result from the segmentation of the 19 bright-field images of healthy brain organoids from the largest public dataset available [14]. Images are acquired at 9 days (7 images), 14 days (6 images) and 15 days of culture (6 images). These images were segmented with a U-Net framework trained with a classical data augmentation strategy [6,22]. All scripts are written in python.

2.2 TDA

We based our implementation on the Ripser algorithms as it outperforms others codes in computation times and memory efficiency and proposes a Vietoris-Rips filtration step [2,25]. We perform TDA on each image by first computing the Persistence Homology (PH). PH maps a set of points P with a distance function F to retrieve topological features in segmented images.

To summarize this approach, a $S_d(P)$ space is defined by all points within the distance d (a disc centered in P with a d radius) from a point p in P. A connection is equal to two discs overlapping in the same topological space. If d is small, the number of connected components (C) in the space is equal to p in P, while if d increase, C is equal to one. Thus, for a given d, the topological feature vector associated contains shape information and the aim is to study them [7–9].

A barcode encodes the topological feature evolution. The beginning of a bar represents the "birth" of a feature. All zero-dimensional features are "born" at zero and their length represents the non-static nature of the clustering. The largest code is the most persistent feature. The connected components are sorted by increasing d value. Lower d correspond to high components similarities [9,12].

Persistence diagrams describing data structures can also be used to compare PH. A point in this diagram represents a topological feature according to its' birth (abscesses) and death (ordinate). We plot zero-dimensional and one-dimensional topological features, respectively H0 and H1. H0 represents the connected components of the point cloud; H1 corresponds to holes and informs about dynamics [20]. We compare the PH of brain organoid images at different developmental stages of these cultures.

2.3   Clustering Feature Vectors

We cluster the feature vector points from the persistence diagrams [27]. Our goal is to observe if H0 and H1 feature clustering are identical; if some clusters, representing the structure of brain organoids are linked to each other; if the clustering varies according to the developmental stage. We implement clustering both with kmeans [21] and with a SVM [11] and obtained identical clustering in all cases. We thus refer to the algorithm generically as "the clustering algorithm". To automatically select the number of clusters k, we calculate elbow points on inertia curves [19]: we retrieve the distance between each data point and its centroid, squaring this distance, and summing these squares across a cluster for all the dataset. k equals to 4 for H0 and H1 at each developmental stage.

2.4   Quantitative Comparisons

To compare the persistence diagrams we first perform a linear regression on the H1 point clouds [1]. Then we compute the average point cloud entropy [4], dispersion [26], and persistence [19] for each developmental stage and for each cluster within each developmental stage. We also compute the pairwise Wasserstein distance between developmental stages and between clusters [3].

We compare each feature vector in the same statistical space with a t-distributed Stochastic Neighbor Embedding (t-SNE). t-SNE preserves the local dataset structure by minimizing the divergence between two distributions respective to the map point locations [15]. An asymmetric probability based on dissimilarities is calculated between an object and its probable neighbor [15]. We choose the effective number of local neighbors as the number of clusters points. To match distributions in a low dimensional space, we aim at minimizing a Kullback-Leibler (K-L) cost function such as in [17]. One-degree freedom Student t-distribution avoids the crowding issue [17]. We reduce iterations with momentum. To compare feature vectors representation, we calculate the K-L divergence between groups.

3   Results

3.1   Qualitative

Global barcodes and persistence diagrams for each stage of brain organoid cultures are shown Fig. 2. For each developmental stage we show a global representation, instead of sample barcodes and persistence diagrams corresponding to an individual input image. Barcode patterns differ between each developmental stage. Bars at 9 days are shorter than from 14 and 15 days. This reveals a most persistent H1 feature of the point cloud at later stages, whereas H0 features are similar between groups. H0 and H1 features of persistence diagrams seems less dispersed at 9 days than for later stages.

To further compare feature vector distributions between groups we combine TDA with clustering. H0 and H1 clustering seems different in term of point proportions and positions according to the stage of culture. To quantify these observations, we calculate several metrics on H0 and H1 features.

3.2   Quantitative

In this section all calculations are made on the individual feature vectors for all images and rendered as a mean. We calculate the linear regression on the H1 feature diagrams. Table 1 shows the slope and intercept of these linear regressions, as well as the entropy, dispersion, and average persistence for each developmental stage. We also compute the pairwise average Wasserstein distance between features for each developmental stage.

The linear regression for H1 at 9 days is markedly different from that at 14 and 15 days. The entropy for H1 at 14 days is slightly higher than for 9 and 15 days. All other parameters are quite close within H0 and H1 for all three developmental stages. We calculate the average Wasserstein distance between all points in every pair of developmental stage. For H0, distances are greater for 15 days than for 9 or 14 days. For H1, 14 days has the biggest distance with others groups and within itself.

Table 2 shows the point distribution across clusters (in percentage) and the entropy within clusters for each developmental stage for H0 and H1. For H0, the entropy is greater for C1 clusters and lower for clusters further from the origin, for all three groups. For H1, the entropy is greater for C0 clusters and lower for C1 clusters. For both H0 and H1 features, the percentage of points in a persistence diagram constituting a cluster is largest at C0 for the earliest stages and the lowest for C1. The differences are attenuated at the latest stage for H1.

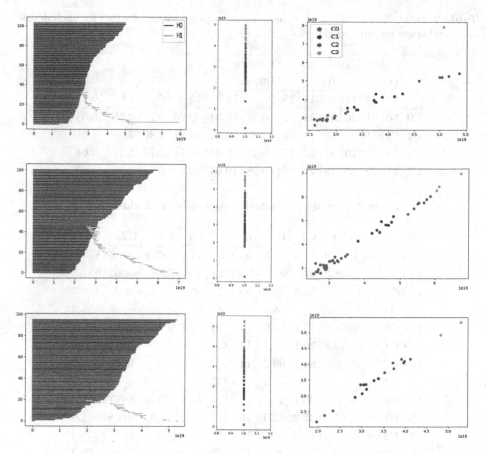

Fig. 2. Average representation for each developmental stage of barcode and H0 and H1 persistence diagrams. First row: 9 days. Second row: 14 days. Third row: 15 days. For this figure, average barcode and persistence clustering diagrams are calculated from the individual representations for each input image.

Table 1. Slope and intercept from the linear regression; entropy, dispersion and average persistence for each developmental stage; pairwise average Wasserstein distance between each developmental stage.

	Linear reg.		Entropy	Dispersion	Average	Wasserstein distance		
	Slope	Intercept		$(\times 10^{34})$	persistence	9	14	15
H0 9	–	–	47.92	9.82	5.38×10^{17}	561 222	579 195	609 972
H0 14	–	–	47.93	10.07	5.44×10^{17}	–	597 156	627 910
H0 15	–	–	47.93	10.23	5.48×10^{17}	–	–	658 625
H1 9	0.6	704	10.46	9.82	869.82	633	656	632
H1 14	1.1	304	12.26	10.69	865.65	–	672	651
H1 15	1.4	208	9.31	10.23	825.50	–	–	617

Table 2. Point distribution across clusters and entropy within clusters for each developmental stage for H0 and H1.

	Points (%)						Entropy					
	H0			H1			H0			H1		
	9	14	15	9	14	15	9	14	15	9	14	15
C0	50	51	46	42	39	27	10.33	10.34	10.23	9.72	9.39	10.03
C1	1	1	1	13	13	24	44.21	44.21	44.21	4.40	2.56	4.21
C2	18	21	20	27	27	17	9.41	9.89	9.51	5.78	5.41	4.64
C3	31	27	33	18	21	32	9.98	10.01	9.96	6.18	3.20	4.83

Table 3. Average Wasserstein distance between clusters.

H0	C0	C1	C2	C3	H1	C0	C1	C2	C3
9 - C0	43.5	45.0	54.9	52.3	9 - C0	45.5	183.2	561.6	870.7
9 - C1	–	38.2	47.6	50.6	9 - C1	–	55.8	478.5	687.5
9 - C2	–	–	54.8	58.9	9 - C2	–	–	31.3	488.5
9 - C3	–	–	–	58.7	9 - C3	–	–	–	53.2
14 - C0	71.8	74.9	70.7	74.9	14 - C0	53.9	235.3	520.4	965.7
14 - C1	–	73.8	70.1	72.7	14 - C1	–	51.9	401.1	750.3
14 - C2	–	–	66.2	69.2	14 - C2	–	–	48.7	531.2
14 - C3	–	–	–	71.3	14 - C3	–	–	–	71.5
15 - C0	50.1	59.5	30.7	44.8	15 - C0	47.4	138.0	546.7	706.3
15 - C1	–	61.9	37.2	53.9	15 - C1	–	44.0	408.8	568.4
15 - C2	–	–	18.0	26.5	15 - C2	–	–	35.1	439.9
15 - C3	–	–	–	38.0	15 - C3	–	–	–	55.2

We calculate the average pairwise point to point Wasserstein distance between clusters to them within a persistence diagram, see Table 3. For H0 features, there is no pair of feature that is consistently the furthest or the closest over time. However, the average distance between clusters is greatest at 14 days. For H1, the distance between clusters is strikingly bigger than that within clusters. The distances are also greater at 14 days, especially for C3.

Table 4 shows the Wasserstein distances within each cluster for each developmental stage. The distance is greatest at 15 days for H0 and at 14 days for H1. To analyze the variability and potential prediction of an image, we compare persistence feature vectors in the same statistical space using t-SNE, see Table 5. For H0, distances between and within groups are near. For H1, the distance between 14 and 15 days is markedly greater than all other distances.

Figure 3 shows the K-L divergence between developmental stages and clusters. For H0, the divergence between clusters of different groups is much bigger than that within a group. For H1 the biggest divergences are for certain clusters at 14 days.

Table 4. Wasserstein distances within each cluster for each developmental stage.

HO ($\times 10^{19}$)	9	14	15	H1 ($\times 10^{19}$)	9	14	15
C0	0.99	0.26	3.04	C0	1.06	2.89	2.25
C1	1.40	0.93	4.58	C1	1.47	3.78	3.19
C2	1.84	1.65	5.63	C2	2.15	6.50	3.92
C3	2.29	2.27	6.43	C3	2.67	5.12	5.08

Table 5. K-L divergence between developmental stages for HO and H1 feature vectors reduced by t-SNE.

HO ($\times 10^{19}$)	9	14	15	H1	9	14	15
9		2.83	2.81	2.75	9	3886	1215	2648
14		–	3.23	2.85	14	–	3682	5741
15		–	–	2.76	15	–	–	2556

4   Discussion

Our aim is to automatically characterize brain organoid morphology according to the step of culture using TDA-clustering. The TDA pattern of brain organoids and their feature clusters evolve according to the developmental stage. The persistence diagram of early cultures approaches a right line characterized by a lower slope and higher intercept than that of later cultures. The clustering strategy strengthens the characterization of developmental groups by showing differences in distances and entropy in inter-intra groups. Dimensional reduction on clustered feature vectors confirms the particularity of the 14th day.

There is an evolution in the persistence diagram over the culture development which could be linked to neuroepithelial formation, a crucial event that occurs before 14 days of culture [13]. Our goal is to find a single representation of images by persistence diagram that characterize this formation which is usually determined by the calculation of multiple morphological indexes [5].

To verify these qualitative results, we calculate parameters currently used to compare persistence diagram representations [1,3,4,19,26]. All parameters, except the dispersion and persistence average, seem to support the qualitative results. The slope and entropy increase with later stage while the intercept decreases. The Wasserstein distance between feature points representations evolves between early and later stages. An other calculation of dispersion and persistence average, based upon the difference of distribution inside cluster proposed in [19], could be used to see if such difference persist in future studies.

To further analyze the feature point distributions of persistence diagrams from brain organoid images, we observe TDA with two clustering methodologies [11,27]. Instead of applying clustering on the overall feature vectors [19], we segregate HO and H1 vectors. As SVM render same clustering as kmeans, we calculate the parameters on clusters from each persistence diagrams once. Analysis

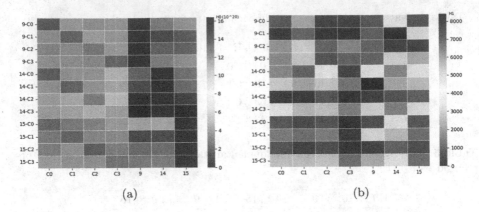

Fig. 3. K-L divergences between developmental stages and clusters for H0 (a) and H1 (b) feature vectors reduced by t-SNE.

of feature cluster representations at various days, allows to further characterize the brain organoid morphology pattern. Some clusters are characterized by extreme metric values. The relation between the clusters and the morphological characteristics of the segmented images must still be explored.

The groups clusters comparison, based upon feature vectors constituting the diagrams, needs to be further studied. We could also try other dimensional reduction methodologies or, propose a better classification of feature clustering, based on a Random forest classifier on persistence images [10]. An other topic to explore is the comparison of TDA-clustering strategies with classical shape analysis on brain organoid cultures (index calculation such as perimeter, surfaces...) or others strategies usually calculated on biomedical images [5,18,24]. When TDA-clustering strategy will be validated on other brain organoid image datasets, such automatic methodologies could help follow the growth of these cultures, predict their developmental stage, or compare physio-pathological models [5].

5   Conclusion

We propose using TDA-clustering to characterize the morphological development of brain organoids. TDA-clustering allows us to highlight some patterns verified by the calculation of parameters on persistence diagrams and this both with kmeans and SVM clustering. The evolution of the TDA representation seems to appear before 14 days of culture and, could be linked to neuroepithelial formations. t-SNE analysis applied on TDA-clustering feature vectors suggests such strategy could help the developmental stage prediction of segmented images. Future work will include putting these clusters in relation with the corresponding morphological characteristics of the segmented images.

References

1. Baas, N.A., Carlsson, G.E., Quick, G., Szymik, M., Thaule, M. (eds.): Topological Data Analysis. AS, vol. 15. Springer, Cham (2020). https://doi.org/10.1007/978-3-030-43408-3
2. Bauer, U.: Ripser: efficient computation of Vietoris–Rips persistence barcodes. J. Appl. Comput. Topology **5**(3), 391–423 (2021). https://doi.org/10.1007/s41468-021-00071-5
3. Berwald, J.J., Gottlieb, J.M., Munch, E.: Computing wasserstein distance for persistence diagrams on a quantum computer. (2018). arXiv: 1809.06433
4. Bouleux, G., Dugast, M., Marcon, E.: Information topological characterization of periodically correlated processes by dilation operators. IEEE Trans. Inf. Theory **65**(10), 6484–6495 (2019). https://doi.org/10.1109/TIT.2019.2923217
5. Brémond Martin, C., Simon Chane, C., Clouchoux, C., Histace, A.: Recent trends and perspectives in cerebral organoids imaging and analysis. Front. Neurosci. **15**, 629067 (2021). https://doi.org/10.3389/fnins.2021.629067
6. Brémond Martin, C., Simon Chane, C., Clouchoux, C., Histace, A.: Aaegan loss optimizations supporting data augmentation on cerebral organoid bright-field images. In: Proceedings of the 17th International Joint Conference on Computer Vision, Imaging and Computer Graphics Theory and Applications, VISIGRAPP 2022 4, pp. 307–314 (2022)
7. Edelsbrunner, L.: Zomorodian: topological persistence and simplification. Discrete Comput. Geom. **28**(4), 511–533 (2002). https://doi.org/10.1007/s00454-002-2885-2
8. Edelsbrunner, H., Harer, J.: Persistent homology-a survey. In: Goodman, J.E., Pach, J., Pollack, R. (eds.) Contemporary Mathematics, vol. 453, pp. 257–282. American Mathematical Society, Providence, Rhode Island (2008). https://doi.org/10.1090/conm/453/08802
9. Edelsbrunner, H., Harer, J.: Computational Topology, p. 294. American Mathematical Society, Providence (2010)
10. Frahi, T., Argerich, C., Yun, M., Falco, A., Barasinski, A., Chinesta, F.: Tape surfaces characterization with persistence images. AIMS Mater. Sci. **7**(4), 364–380 (2020). https://doi.org/10.3934/matersci.2020.4.364
11. García, E., Lozano, F.: Boosting Support Vector Machines. In: Mldm Posters, pp. 153–167 (2007)
12. Ghrist, R.: Barcodes: the persistent topology of data. Bull. Am. Math. Soc. **45**(01), 61–76 (2007). https://doi.org/10.1090/S0273-0979-07-01191-3
13. Giandomenico, S.L., Sutcliffe, M., Lancaster, M.A.: Generation and long-term culture of advanced cerebral organoids for studying later stages of neural development. Nat. Protoc. **16**(2), 579–602 (2021). https://doi.org/10.1038/s41596-020-00433-w
14. Gomez-Giro, G., et al.: Synapse alterations precede neuronal damage and storage pathology in a human cerebral organoid model of CLN3-juvenile neuronal ceroid lipofuscinosis. Acta Neuropathol. Commun. **7**(1), 222 (2019). https://doi.org/10.1186/s40478-019-0871-7
15. Hinton, G., Roweis, S.: Stochastic neighbor embedding. In: Advances in Neural Information Processing Systems, pp. 857–864 (2003)
16. Kelava, I., Lancaster, M.A.: Dishing out mini-brains: current progress and future prospects in brain organoid research. Dev. Biol. **420**(2), 199–209 (2016). https://doi.org/10.1016/j.ydbio.2016.06.037

17. van der Maaten, L., Hinton, G.: Visualizing data using TSNE. J. Mach. Learn. Res. **9**(1), 2579–2605 (2008)
18. Mingqiang, Y., Kidiyo, K., Joseph, R.: A Survey of Shape Feature Extraction Techniques. In: Yin, P.Y. (ed.) Pattern Recognition Techniques, Technology and Applications. InTech (Nov 2008)
19. Nguyen, N.K.K., Bui, M.: Detecting anomalies in the dynamics of a market index with topological data analysis. Int. J. Syst. Innov. **6**(6), 14 (2021)
20. Otter, N., Porter, M.A., Tillmann, U., Grindrod, P., Harrington, H.A.: A roadmap for the computation of persistent homology. EPJ Data Sci. **6**(1), 17 (2017). https://doi.org/10.1140/epjds/s13688-017-0109-5
21. Panagopoulos, D.: Topological data analysis and clustering (2022). arXiv: 2201.09054
22. Ronneberger, O., Fischer, P., Brox, T.: U-Net: convolutional networks for biomedical image segmentation (2015). arXiv: 1505.04597
23. Skaf, Y., Laubenbacher, R.: Topological data analysis in biomedicine: a review. J. Biomed. Inform. **130**, 104082 (2022). https://doi.org/10.1016/j.jbi.2022.104082
24. Thibault, G.: Shape and texture indexes application to cell nuclei classification. Int. J. Pattern Recognit. Artif. Intell. **27**(01), 1357002 (2013)
25. Tralie, C., Saul, N., Bar-On, R.: Ripser. py: a lean persistent homology library for python. J. Open Source Softw. **3**(29), 925 (2018)
26. Turner, K.: Medians of populations of persistence diagrams. Homology Homotopy Appl. **22**(1), 255–282 (2020). https://doi.org/10.4310/HHA.2020.v22.n1.a15
27. Yang, B., Fu, X., Sidiropoulos, N.D., Hong, M.: Towards K-means-friendly spaces: simultaneous deep learning and clustering (2017). arXiv: 1610.04794

Fetal Cortex Segmentation with Topology and Thickness Loss Constraints

Liu Li[1](✉), Qiang Ma[1], Zeju Li[1], Cheng Ouyang[1], Weitong Zhang[1],
Anthony Price[2], Vanessa Kyriakopoulou[2], Lucilio C. Grande[2],
Antonis Makropoulos[2], Joseph Hajnal[2], Daniel Rueckert[1,3], Bernhard Kainz[1,4],
and Amir Alansary[1]

[1] BioMedIA Group, Department of Computing, Imperial College London,
London, UK
liu.li20@imperial.ac.uk
[2] King's College, London, UK
[3] Technical University of Munich, Munich, Germany
[4] FAU Erlangen-Nürnberg, Erlangen, Germany

Abstract. The segmentation of the fetal cerebral cortex from magnetic resonance imaging (MRI) is an important tool for neurobiological research about the developing human brain. Manual segmentation is difficult and time-consuming. Limited image resolution and partial volume effects introduce errors and labeling noise when attempting to automate the process through machine learning. The significant morphological changes observed during brain growth pose additional challenges for learning-based image segmentation methods, which may drastically increase the amount of necessary training data. In this paper, we propose a framework to learn from noisy labels by using additional regularization via shape priors for the accurate segmentation of the cortical gray matter (CGM) in 3D. Firstly, we introduce a novel structure consistency loss based on persistent homology analysis of the cortical topology. Secondly, a regularization loss term is proposed by integrating assumptions about the cortical thickness within each sample. Our experiments on the developing human connectome project (dHCP) dataset show that our method can predict accurate CGM segmentation learned from noisy labels.

1 Introduction

Quantification and visualisation of the development of cortical gray matter (CGM) from magnetic resonance imaging (MRI) is an important step for the study of the developing human brain. During the perinatal period, the cortex develops rapidly from a smooth to a highly convoluted surface [4]. Compared to brain MR imaging in adults, the scanned fetal brain images are lower in contrast and resolution, and prone to severe motion artifacts. In addition, the small size of the fetal brains compared to adult brains and limitations regarding the

---

Supplementary Information The online version contains supplementary material available at https://doi.org/10.1007/978-3-031-23223-7_11.

J. S. H. Baxter et al. (Eds.): EPIMI 2022/ML-CDS 2022/TDA4BiomedicalImaging 2022,
LNCS 13755, pp. 123–133, 2022.
https://doi.org/10.1007/978-3-031-23223-7_11

124   L. Li et al.

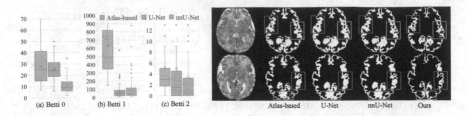

Fig. 1. Motivation. Left: Betti errors of the CGM segmentation in three different methods (the lower, the better). Right: Over-segmentation along with imaging artifacts.

length of the image acquisition further restrict the resolution and contrast of fetal MRIs. Recent fetal motion correction and super-resolution methods [1,13,17,24] in combination with fast imaging methods can reconstruct a 3D volume of the fetal brain sufficiently well for analysis. However, partial volume effects caused by high motion and large slice distances can still persist and cause blurry CGM boundaries especially for older fetal brains, *i.e.*, gestational ages (GA) over 30 weeks. Given artifact-prone MRI data, the performance of standard deep learning segmentation approaches, *e.g.*, using U-Net [23] or nnU-Net [12] approaches that largely rely on the image contrast, often results in inaccurate segmentation. Meanwhile, manual labeling of fetal 3D brain scans is extremely time-consuming with significant high intra- and inter-observer errors. As a result, there are only few publicly available fetal brain datasets with comprehensive ground truth segmentations [21].

Contribution: In this paper we leverage automatically generated segmentation labels from an atlas-based EM tissue segmentation [19] as *weak supervision*, and further propose two new shape constraints to regularize 3D segmentation during training to account for potential segmentation errors in the training data. The proposed constraints are derived from the required consistency of the topological structure of the CGM across the fetal cortex and the consistency of cortical thickness within each fetus. Specifically, despite the large shape variability of fetal brains across different age groups, the topology of the CGM is invariant, *i.e.*, the structure of CGM should be a connected surface without any holes or interjections. This topology invariance can be specified by Betti numbers [30], defined as a vector $\beta = (\beta_0, \beta_1, \beta_2)$ of which the k'th element β_k is corresponding to the number of holes in dimension k. β_0, β_1 and β_2 refer to the number of connected components, loops or holes, and hollow voids, respectively. Note that we only consider $k \leq 2$ in 3D images and that $\beta_k = 0$ when $k > 2$. For an ideal CGM surface, its Betti number should be $\beta = (1, 0, 1)$. However, as shown in Fig. 1-left, the Betti number of three different baseline methods are very high in all three dimensions, indicating the existing methods have severe topological errors for CGM segmentation. We therefore propose a self-supervised topological loss term based on persistent homology (PH) analysis [11]. We show that the introduction of this term can reduce topological errors of the predicted labels leading to a better segmentation.

Our second contribution addresses the over-segmentation problem which occurs often when the input MRI has significant amounts of partial volume artifacts. This is more likely to occur in older fetuses because of the higher complexity of the cortical surfaces and folding. Figure 1-right displays the over-segmented regions. We observed that distance between inner and outer CGM boundary is much thicker for the over-segmentation regions than other regions. To address this we propose a second regularization term that constrains the consistency of cortical thickness and thus alleviates the over-segmentation problem caused by imaging artifacts. This constraint is based on the anatomical prior that the thickness of CGM changes within a limited range around 1–4 mm on average for different fetal brain regions [29]. We demonstrate the performance of these two shape-based regularization terms on a large dataset of 274 fetal MR images ranging from 20.6 to 38.2 weeks GA. The results show that the additional shape constraints can improve the CGM segmentation significantly compared to existing methods in terms of topological correctness and number of cases with over-segmentation.

Related Work: Automatic fetal brain segmentation methods in the literature can be categorized into two main groups, namely atlas-based [18,19] and deep learning-based methods [7,16,21]. The former leverage shape priors from anatomical or probabilistic atlases to segment images by registering and propagating labels from the atlas template to the target image. The shape prior here is explicitly introduced by constraining the smoothness of the deformation field between the atlas and the target image. However, the registration process requires several rounds of pair-wised optimization, which is time-consuming and lacks robustness if the anatomical difference between atlas and subject are large. In particular, the registration of the cortical geometry from atlas to subject is challenging due to the large cortical variability. Recently, deep learning-based registration methods have been proposed to improve the registration efficiency [3,26]. However, such models can only learn the statistical distribution for the deformation field across a population of subjects, without localized pair-wise optimization for the atlas and target image. Thus, a trade-off between the registration efficiency and accuracy remains. On the other hand, typical deep learning-based segmentation methods, often using a U-Net as backbone [7,16,21], rely on supervision with extensive amounts of manually generated segmentation masks for training [7,21]. Recently, topological priors have been introduced to encourage the generation of segmentation masks with an expected topology [5,6,10,11]. However, these methods are designed for cardiac segmentation, exhibiting simple shape priors and accurate ground truth labels. To the best of our knowledge, we are the first to introduce topology constraints for 3D cortex segmentation.[1]

2 Method

Two self-supervised shape loss constraints – topology $\mathcal{L}_{\text{Topo}}$ and thickness $\mathcal{L}_{\text{Thick}}$ – are proposed in order to learn from weak training labels and to introduce a-priori assumptions. Our approach can be used with any segmentation-network. In this paper, we choose a default U-Net as a baseline architecture.

2.1 Topology Constraint: The CGM of fetuses over 30 weeks GA develops rapidly from being smooth to becoming highly convoluted [2]. Despite these

---

[1] Code is available at: https://github.com/smilell/FetalTopology.

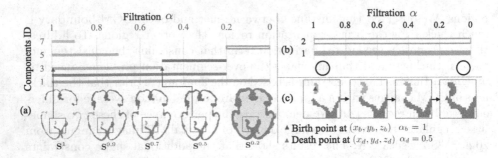

Fig. 2. (a) Persistence barcode for **predicted probability** map **S**. Each bar represents a topology component corresponding to the region with the same color in the binary segmentation map $\mathbf{S}^\alpha$. The horizontal coordinate of each bar is the birth and death filtration α of this topology, and the length of each bar is the lifetime of this topology component. The solid bars represent connected components, while the void bar represents the component with holes. (b) Persistence barcode of the **ground truth** binary map, which is invariable across the changing filtration level α. (c) An selected area to show the topology changes of the light blue component.

rapid shape changes, its topological structure should be invariant as a *connected surface*. Following [5,11], we include the topological loss term through PH analysis [8]. Different from [11] which encourages the topology similarity between prediction and ground truth, our method encourages topology of the predicted CGM to be similar to a sphere.

Given a 3D MR image $\mathbf{I}$ with a size of $N_x \times N_y \times N_z$, of which element $I_{x,y,z} \in \mathbb{R}$ at coordinate (x, y, z), a segmentation network parameterized by ω predicts the segmentation probability map by $\mathbf{S} = f(\mathbf{I}; \omega)$, with its element $S_{x,y,z} \in [0, 1]$. The binary segmentation result $\mathbf{S}^\alpha$ is decided by its decision threshold α with its element $S_{x,y,z}^\alpha = \mathbb{1}(S_{x,y,z} \geq \alpha)$. Here, $\mathbb{1}$ is an indicator function which is equal to 1 if and only if $S_{x,y,z} \geq \alpha$, where α is a decision threshold, which is also called *filtration*. Given $\mathbf{S}^\alpha$, the topological structure can be modeled by cubical complex for further topology analysis[2].

2.1.1 Preliminaries: Two major tools for topology analysis are PH [8] and Betti numbers. Here we choose PH, which is a better method to analyze the topology, as it can take all the $\alpha \in [1, 0]$ into account and measure the persistence or stability of the topology components, while Betti number only measures the topology complexity under certain α [9]. The result of PH analysis can be visualized using the persistence barcode [9], which records all the topology changes across different filtration α, as shown in Fig. 2. When filtration level α decreases from 1 to 0, more voxels are involved in the predicted segmentation $\mathbf{S}^\alpha$, and the topological structure of each components on the prediction segmentation is born or dies at different α's. Here we denote the filtration when a component is born

---

[2] Although simplicial complex is widely used in general topology analysis [30], modeling the images by a cubical complex will simplify the calculation due to the inherent cubical structure of the image [27].

and dies as α_b and α_d. For example, the blue component, as shown in Fig. 2 (c), is born at $\alpha_b = 1$ and dies at $\alpha_d = 0.5$. We further define the value of $\alpha_b - \alpha_d$ as the lifetime of this component. The component with longer lifetime is more persistent. Moreover, the number of bars in dimension n at each α is the Betti number β_n^α, e.g., the purple and navy components merges into the gray component at $\alpha = 0.2$ to form a connected component with a hole, so that there are two bars (one solid and one void) that exist from $\alpha = 0.2$ to $\alpha = 0$, accounting for $\beta_0 = 1$ and $\beta_1 = 1$, respectively.

2.1.2 Optimization: In practice, we use the Cubical Ripser [14] package to calculate the PH [27]. After accessing the birth α_b and death point α_d of each component in the persistence barcode [11], we aim to encourage the topology of the predicted CGM segmentation to be consistently the same as that of *a sphere* across different filtrations α's. Our goal can be realized by increasing the similarity of two corresponding persistence barcodes. The persistence barcodes of predicted segmentation and a sphere are shown in Fig. 2 (a) and (b), respectively. We propose to optimize the problem with three steps:

1. We first make assumptions about the topology of ground truth segmentation and define the desired Betti number β, which is $(1, 0, 1)$ in this study.
2. Among the total q_n topology components in dimension n of the predicted segmentation $\mathbf{S}$ across different α, we choose the most persistent β_n components which have the longest lifetime. In order to encourage the similarity between the two persistence barcodes, we increase the lifetime of all the chosen β_n persistent components, i.e., $\max(\alpha_b - \alpha_d)$, which is equivalent to optimizing $\alpha_b \to 1$ and $\alpha_d \to 0$.
3. We eliminate the rest $q_n - \beta_n$ components which are not chosen for each dimension by decreasing their lifetime, i.e., $\min(\alpha_b - \alpha_d)$, which is equivalent to optimizing $\alpha_b = \alpha_d$.

As shown in Fig. 2 (c), the light blue component is first born at the coordinate of (x_b, y_b, z_b) and then merged into the gray component at (x_d, y_d, z_d). The filtration α_b, thus, is the predicted segmentation probability at (x_b, y_b, z_b) that $\alpha_b = S_{x_b,y_b,z_b}$. Similarly, $\alpha_d = S_{x_d,y_d,z_d}$. Therefore, we can change the lifetime of each topology components by optimizing the predicted probability at (x_d, y_d, z_d) and (x_b, y_b, z_b). Specifically, we build a vector for all the birth points $\mathbf{S}^{n,b}$ consisting of q_n elements, where n is the topology dimension. Its ith element $S_i^{n,b}$ is the value of segmentation probability S_{x_b,y_b,z_b}, which equals to α_b for i^{th} topology component. Similarly, $\mathbf{S}^{n,d}$ is defined for all the death points. The order of the elements in $\mathbf{S}^{n,b}$ and $\mathbf{S}^{n,d}$ is paired and sorted in descending order according to the length of lifetime of $S_i^{n,b} - S_i^{n,d}$. The final topology loss term can be formulated as the sum of topology loss from all dimension: $\mathcal{L}_{\text{Topo}} = \sum_{n=1}^{3} \mathcal{L}_n$, where the loss in each dimension n is calculated as:

$$\mathcal{L}_n = \underbrace{\sum_{i=1}^{\beta_n}(\|S_i^{n,b} - 1\|_2^2 + \|S_i^{n,d} - 0\|_2^2)}_{\text{encouraging the persistent components}} + \underbrace{(\sum_{i=\beta_n}^{q_n} 2\|S_i^{n,b} - S_i^{n,d}\|_2^2)}_{\text{eliminating the other components}}. \quad (1)$$

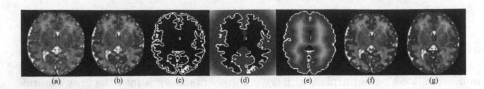

Fig. 3. The process of generating self-supervised pseudo labelmaps. (a) MR image **I**, (b) segmentation prediction, (c) binary CGM surface **C**, (d) distance map for inner surface Φ^{in} (orange regions corresponding to larger values), (e) distance map for outer surface Φ^{out}, (f) red: inner region $\mathbf{Z}^{in}$ and blue: inner surface $\mathbf{C}^{in}$, (g) red: outer region $\mathbf{Z}^{out}$ and blue: outer surface $\mathbf{C}^{out}$. (Color figure online)

2.2 Thickness Constraint: We propose the second constraint that is based on the a priori knowledge about the thickness of CGM [29] to avoid over-segmentation. During the training process, two pseudo label maps $\mathbf{Z}_{in}$ and $\mathbf{Z}_{out}$ are generated as additional ground truth to constrain the thickness of the predicted CGM segmentation. Here $\mathbf{Z}_{in}$ refers to the region within certain distance to the inner surface, and $\mathbf{Z}_{out}$ refers to the region within another distance to the outer surface. This process consists of three steps as shown in Fig. 3: (1) Detecting the inner surface $\mathbf{C}_{in}$ and outer surface $\mathbf{C}_{out}$ by Sobel operator; (2) Calculating the mean distance from inner to outer surface d_{in} and from outer to inner surface d_{in}; (3) Generating $\mathbf{Z}_{in}$ and $\mathbf{Z}_{out}$ for self-supervised training.

Specifically, in the first step, given the predicted CGM segmentation map $\mathbf{S}$, we use a convolution layer with a 3D Sobel kernel [15] to detect the surface of CGM $\mathbf{S^c}$ with its element $S^c_{x,y,z} \in \mathbb{R}$. Then, the continuous surface $\mathbf{S^c}$ is binarized to $\mathbf{C}$ (with its element $C_{x,y,z}$) with a threshold t: $C_{x,y,z} = \mathbb{1}(S^c_{x,y,z} \geq t)$. After that, the binary CGM surface map $\mathbf{C}$ is further split into the inner surface $\mathbf{C}^{in}$ (with its element $C^{in}_{x,y,z}$) and outer surface $\mathbf{C}^{out}$ (with its element $C^{out}_{x,y,z}$). The split criterion is: Given a voxel (x, y, z) from the cortex surface where $C_{x,y,z} = 1$, if this voxel is adjacent with cerebrospinal fluid, skull or background, then $C^{in}_{x,y,z} = 0$ and $C^{out}_{x,y,z} = 1$, otherwise $C^{in}_{x,y,z} = 1$ and $C^{out}_{x,y,z} = 0$.

In the second step, the mean distance from inner to outer surface d_{in} is calculated by the inner distance map Φ^{in}. Its element $\phi^{in}_{x,y,z} \in \mathbb{R}$ is the Euclidean distance of a pixel at (x, y, z) to the closest boundary point of the inner surface $C^{in}_{x,y,z}$. We set $\phi^{in}_{x,y,z}$ to be zero for pixels inside $C^{in}_{x,y,z}$. $C^{out}_{x,y,z}$ is calculated in a similar manner. Given Φ^{in} and $\mathbf{C}^{out}$, Φ^{out} and $\mathbf{C}^{in}$, the mean distance from inner to outer surface d_{in} can be calculated as:

$$d_{in} = \frac{1}{N} \sum_{x,y,z} \phi^{in}_{x,y,z} \mathbb{1}(C^{out}_{x,y,z} = 1), \tag{2}$$

where $N = \sum_{x,y,z} \mathbb{1}(C^{out}_{x,y,z} = 1)$ represents the number of all the voxels on the CGM outer surface. We also calculate d_{out} in a similar way.

In the third step, we calculate the inner region $\mathbf{Z}^{in}$ with its element $Z^{in}_{x,y,z}$:

$$Z^{in}_{x,y,z} = \mathbb{1}(\phi^{in}_{x,y,z} \leq d_{in}). \tag{3}$$

Similarly, the outer region $\mathbf{Z}^{out}$ can be defined as $Z^{out}_{x,y,z} = \mathbb{1}(\phi^{out}_{x,y,z} \leq d_{out})$. The thickness loss is designed with two parts, constraining the prediction CGM to be simultaneously within certain distance from the inner and outer surfaces:

$$\mathcal{L}_{Thick} = \lambda_{in}\mathcal{L}_{CE}(\mathbf{S}, \mathbf{Z}^{in}) + \lambda_{out}\mathcal{L}_{CE}(\mathbf{S}, \mathbf{Z}^{out}), \tag{4}$$

where $\mathcal{L}_{CE}$ refers to the cross entropy loss. Overall, the segmentation loss function is a combination of three parts, where $\mathbf{G}$ represents the weak labels generated from DrawEM [20]:

$$\mathcal{L}_R = \mathcal{L}_{CE}(\mathbf{S}, \mathbf{G}) + \lambda_{Topo}\mathcal{L}_{Topo} + \lambda_{Thick}\mathcal{L}_{Thick} \tag{5}$$

3   Evaluation and Results

Dataset: Our experiments are conducted on 274 fetal MRI scans (corresponding to 253 subjects) with a GA ranging from 20.6 to 38.2 weeks as part of the dHCP project. The dataset was acquired by a Philips Achieva 3T system using single shot turbo spin echo (ssTSE) sequence with acquisition resolution = $1.1 \times 1.1 \times 2.2\,mm$ [22]. All scanned images were motion corrected and reconstructed to $0.5 \times 0.5 \times 0.5\,mm$ for the fetal head region of interest (ROI), and reoriented to a common coordinate system [13,17,28].

These images are randomly split into 202 training, 18 validation and 54 test samples, without overlap. Before training, all the samples are affinely aligned to a 30-week fetal atlas [25] and resized to $128 \times 128 \times 128$. To train and evaluate our method, all the data are pre-processed by the DrawEM methods to obtain weak segmentation labels. 39 slices from 13 MR images are further manually labeled for evaluation. Note that only the weak labels from DrawEM are utilized for training, the manually labeled slices are only used for evaluation.

Setting: The hyper-parameters in Eq. 4 and 5 are experimentally chosen as $\lambda_1 = 2$, $\lambda_2 = 0.5$, $\lambda_{Topo} = 500$ and $\lambda_{Thick} = 2$. Specifically, in Eq. 4, we set λ_1 with a higher value than λ_2 since the CGM inner surface preserves more curves and information than the outer surface, as shown in Fig. 3 (f) and (g). In Eq. 5, the value of λ_{Topo} and λ_2 are chosen so that the three loss terms have a similar order of magnitude. Our proposed method is not restricted to the network structure, we choose a default U-Net as the backbone to compare the performance of varying topology and thickness constraints.

Qualitative Evaluation: We compare our method with two baseline segmentation methods: U-Net [23] and nnU-Net [12] in Fig. 4. Two types of errors can be mitigated by our method, as highlighted in the green and red boxes. First, the topology error of discontinuous CGM segmentation in the green boxes can be fixed by explicitly encouraging correct topology in our method. Second, the red boxes highlight the regions with partial volume effects that cause oversegmentations for all the DrawEM, U-Net and nnU-Net methods. Our thickness and topology constraints visually improve these areas. More segmentation results are shown in the supplementary materials. Note that in this paper we choose the U-Net as the backbone structure, but in principle, our method could be implemented within the nnU-Net framework to further improve performance.

Table 1. Comparison between proposed losses with U-Net and nnU-Net baselines. We use three metrics: Dice score, Betti numbers, and the mean distance to the inner and outer cortical surfaces. The results show that the thickness and topology losses can reduce over-fitting to the weak DrawEM [20] ground truth. ↑: higher, ↓: lower is better.

Method	Dice↑		Betti number↓			Mean distance↓	
	Manual	DrawEM	β_0	β_1	β_2	Inner	Outer
nnU-Net	0.707	**0.867**	10.7	107.1	3.5	3.35	2.43
U-Net	0.707	0.850	25.1	72.8	4.9	3.67	2.69
U-Net + L_{Thick}	0.697	0.824	14.9	60.0	3.4	**3.06**	**2.40**
U-Net + L_{Topo}	0.708	0.847	**6.8**	**15.9**	**2.7**	3.67	2.75
U-Net + L_{Thick} + L_{Topo}	**0.729**	0.840	8.9	29.0	2.9	3.33	2.45

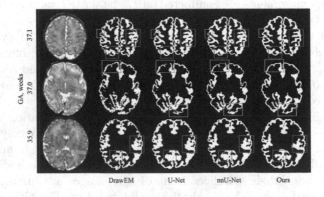

Fig. 4. CGM segmentation results comparison. The green boxes highlight the errors of discontinuous CGM segmentation, and the red boxes highlight the over-segmentation. (Color figure online)

Quantitative Evaluation: The segmentation results are evaluated in terms of three metrics: (1) Dice coefficient similarity (2) Betti number and (3) Mean distance between the inner and outer CGM surface, as shown in Table 1. Our method achieves the best Dice scores when compared to manual segmentations. nn-UNet and U-Net likely overfit DrawEM labels. We also evaluate the topology correctness through Betti numbers. In our case ideal Betti numbers are ($\beta_0 = 1, \beta_1 = 0, \beta_2 = 1$), thus the closer our results are to this triplet, the better. Furthermore, the mean distances of CGM inner surface to outer surface d_{in} and outer to inner surface d_{out} are evaluated. Including the thickness loss term can reduce the mean distance between inner and outer surface and tends to reduce over-segmentation as shown in Fig. 4.

Ablation Study: We train the U-Net by only including the topology constraint or thickness constraint. The segmentation performance decreases, while the performance in terms of Betti numbers or correspondingly mean distance between the inner and outer surface improves, verifying each terms as shown in Table 1.

Discussion: A limitation is that balancing of the two terms can be time-consuming and a hyper-parameter grid search needs to be performed to achieve optimal performance. However, this only needs to be done once for a given image analysis pipeline. Also, the evaluation of topological properties is currently done on the CPU and would likely benefit from parallelization on the GPU.

4   Conclusion

In this paper, we show how to explicitly constrain a cortical segmentation model by introducing topology and thickness constraints. We evaluate our approach on motion-corrected fetal MRI and show improved performance in terms of topological correctness and reduced over-segmentation. In future work we would like to verify our method on other segmentation tasks.

Acknowledgements. Data in this work were provided by ERC Grant Agreement no. [319456]. We are grateful to the families who generously supported this trial.

References

1. Alansary, A., et al.: PVR: patch-to-volume reconstruction for large area motion correction of fetal MRI. IEEE Trans. Med. Imaging **36**(10), 2031–2044 (2017)
2. Arimitsu, T., Shinohara, N., Minagawa, Y., Hoshino, E., Hata, M., Takahashi, T.: Differential age-dependent development of inter-area brain connectivity in term and preterm neonates. Pediatr. Res. **92**, 1017–1025 (2022)
3. Balakrishnan, G., Zhao, A., Sabuncu, M.R., Guttag, J., Dalca, A.V.: VoxelMorph: a learning framework for deformable medical image registration. IEEE Trans. Med. Imaging **38**(8), 1788–1800 (2019)
4. Casey, B., Giedd, J.N., Thomas, K.M.: Structural and functional brain development and its relation to cognitive development. Biol. Psychol. **54**(1–3), 241–257 (2000)
5. Clough, J.R., Byrne, N., Oksuz, I., Zimmer, V.A., Schnabel, J.A., King, A.P.: A topological loss function for deep-learning based image segmentation using persistent homology. arXiv preprint arXiv:1910.01877 (2019)
6. Clough, J.R., Oksuz, I., Byrne, N., Schnabel, J.A., King, A.P.: Explicit topological priors for deep-learning based image segmentation using persistent homology. In: Chung, A.C.S., Gee, J.C., Yushkevich, P.A., Bao, S. (eds.) IPMI 2019. LNCS, vol. 11492, pp. 16–28. Springer, Cham (2019). https://doi.org/10.1007/978-3-030-20351-1_2
7. Dou, H., et al.: A deep attentive convolutional neural network for automatic cortical plate segmentation in fetal MRI. IEEE Trans. Med. Imaging **40**(4), 1123–1133 (2020)
8. Edelsbrunner, H., Harer, J., et al.: Persistent homology-a survey. Contemp. Math. **453**, 257–282 (2008)
9. Ghrist, R.: Barcodes: the persistent topology of data. Bull. Am. Math. Soc. **45**(1), 61–75 (2008)

10. Haft-Javaherian, M., Villiger, M., Schaffer, C.B., Nishimura, N., Golland, P., Bouma, B.E.: A topological encoding convolutional neural network for segmentation of 3D multiphoton images of brain vasculature using persistent homology. In: Proceedings of the IEEE/CVF Conference on Computer Vision and Pattern Recognition Workshops, pp. 990–991 (2020)
11. Hu, X., Li, F., Samaras, D., Chen, C.: Topology-preserving deep image segmentation. Adv. Neural Inf. Process. Syst. **32** (2019)
12. Isensee, F., et al.: nnU-net: self-adapting framework for U-net-based medical image segmentation. arXiv preprint arXiv:1809.10486 (2018)
13. Kainz, B., et al.: Fast volume reconstruction from motion corrupted stacks of 2D slices. IEEE Trans. Med. Imaging **34**(9), 1901–1913 (2015)
14. Kaji, S., Sudo, T., Ahara, K.: Cubical ripser: software for computing persistent homology of image and volume data. arXiv preprint arXiv:2005.12692 (2020)
15. Kanopoulos, N., Vasanthavada, N., Baker, R.L.: Design of an image edge detection filter using the Sobel operator. IEEE J. Solid-State Circuits **23**(2), 358–367 (1988)
16. Khalili, N., et al.: Automatic brain tissue segmentation in fetal MRI using convolutional neural networks. Magn. Reson. Imaging **64**, 77–89 (2019)
17. Kuklisova-Murgasova, M., Quaghebeur, G., Rutherford, M.A., Hajnal, J.V., Schnabel, J.A.: Reconstruction of fetal brain MRI with intensity matching and complete outlier removal. Med. Image Anal. **16**(8), 1550–1564 (2012)
18. Li, L., et al.: CAS-Net: conditional atlas generation and brain segmentation for fetal MRI. In: Sudre, C.H., et al. (eds.) UNSURE/PIPPI -2021. LNCS, vol. 12959, pp. 221–230. Springer, Cham (2021). https://doi.org/10.1007/978-3-030-87735-4_21
19. Makropoulos, A., et al.: Automatic whole brain MRI segmentation of the developing neonatal brain. IEEE Trans. Med. Imaging **33**(9), 1818–1831 (2014)
20. Makropoulos, A., et al.: The developing human connectome project: a minimal processing pipeline for neonatal cortical surface reconstruction. Neuroimage **173**, 88–112 (2018)
21. Payette, K., et al.: An automatic multi-tissue human fetal brain segmentation benchmark using the fetal tissue annotation dataset. Sci. Data **8**(1), 1–14 (2021)
22. Price, A.N., et al.: The developing human connectome project (dHCP): fetal acquisition protocol. In: ISMRM Annual Meeting & Exhibition. vol. 27 (2019)
23. Ronneberger, O., Fischer, P., Brox, T.: U-Net: convolutional networks for biomedical image segmentation. In: Navab, N., Hornegger, J., Wells, W.M., Frangi, A.F. (eds.) MICCAI 2015. LNCS, vol. 9351, pp. 234–241. Springer, Cham (2015). https://doi.org/10.1007/978-3-319-24574-4_28
24. Rousseau, F., et al.: Registration-based approach for reconstruction of high-resolution in utero fetal MR brain images. Acad. Radiol. **13**(9), 1072–1081 (2006)
25. Serag, A., et al.: Construction of a consistent high-definition spatio-temporal atlas of the developing brain using adaptive kernel regression. Neuroimage **59**(3), 2255–2265 (2012)
26. Sinclair, M., et al.: Atlas-ISTN: joint segmentation, registration and atlas construction with image-and-spatial transformer networks. Med. Image Anal. **78**, 102383 (2022)
27. Wagner, H., Chen, C., Vuçini, E.: Efficient computation of persistent homology for cubical data. In: Peikert, R., Hauser, H., Carr, H., Fuchs, R. (eds) Topological Methods in Data Analysis and Visualization II, pp. 91–106. Springer, Heidelberg (2012). https://doi.org/10.1007/978-3-642-23175-9_7

28. Wright, R., et al.: LSTM spatial co-transformer networks for registration of 3D fetal US and MR brain images. In: Melbourne, A., et al. (eds.) PIPPI/DATRA -2018. LNCS, vol. 11076, pp. 149–159. Springer, Cham (2018). https://doi.org/10.1007/978-3-030-00807-9_15
29. Wu, J., et al.: Age-specific structural fetal brain atlases construction and cortical development quantification for Chinese population. Neuroimage **241**, 118412 (2021)
30. Zomorodian, A., Carlsson, G.: Computing persistent homology. Discrete Comput. Geom. **33**(2), 249–274 (2005)

Author Index

Printed in the United States
by Baker & Taylor Publisher Services

Printed in the United States
by Baker & Taylor Publisher Services